Free Video **Free Video**

Essential Test Tips Video from Trivium Test Prep

Dear Customer,

Thank you for purchasing from Trivium Test Prep! We're honored to help you prepare for your exam.

To show our appreciation, we're offering a **FREE *KNAT Essential Test Tips* Video by Trivium Test Prep.*** Our video includes 35 test preparation strategies that will make you successful on your big exam. All we ask is that you email us your feedback and describe your experience with our product. Amazing, awful, or just so-so: we want to hear what you have to say!

To receive your **FREE *KNAT Essential Test Tips* Video**, please email us at 5star@triviumtestprep.com. Include "Free 5 Star" in the subject line and the following information in your email:

1. The title of the product you purchased.
2. Your rating from 1 – 5 (with 5 being the best).
3. Your feedback about the product, including how our materials helped you meet your goals and ways in which we can improve our products.
4. Your full name and shipping address so we can send your **FREE *KNAT Essential Test Tips* Video**.

If you have any questions or concerns please feel free to contact us directly at 5star@triviumtestprep.com.

Thank you!

– Trivium Test Prep Team

*To get access to the free video please email us at 5star@triviumtestprep.com, and please follow the instructions above.

KAPLAN NURSING SCHOOL ENTRANCE EXAM PREP 2024-2025:

1,285 Practice Questions and Study Guide [4th Edition]

E. M. Falgout

TABLE OF CONTENTS

ONLINE RESOURCES

Ascencia Test Prep includes online resources with the purchase of this study guide to help you fully prepare for your Kaplan Nursing School Entrance Exam.

PRACTICE TESTS

In addition to the practice test included in this book, we also offer an online exam. Since many exams today are computer based, practicing your test-taking skills on the computer is a great way to prepare.

REVIEW QUESTIONS

Need more practice? Our review questions use a variety of formats to help you memorize key terms and concepts.

FLASH CARDS

Ascencia Test Prep's flash cards allow you to review important terms easily on your computer or smartphone.

CHEAT SHEETS

Review the core skills you need to master the exam with easy-to-read Cheat Sheets.

FROM STRESS TO SUCCESS

Watch "From Stress to Success," a brief but insightful YouTube video that offers the tips, tricks, and secrets experts use to score higher on the exam.

REVIEWS

Leave a review, send us helpful feedback, or sign up for Ascencia Test Prep promotions—including free books!

Access these materials at: **http://ascenciatestprep.com/knat-online-resources**

INTRODUCTION

Kaplan Nursing School Admissions Test

What Is the Kaplan Nursing School Admissions Test?

The Kaplan Nursing School Admissions Test was developed by Kaplan for use by nursing programs during the application process. The exam evaluates candidates' relevant knowledge and skills so that they can be accurately placed in nursing education programs leading to RN licensure. The Kaplan Nursing School Admissions Test is also used to identify areas in reading, writing, math, and science where nursing students need remediation.

What's on the Kaplan Nursing School Admissions Test?

The Kaplan Nursing School Admissions Test is a multiple-choice test. It tests concepts in reading comprehension, writing, math, and science.

Test	Concepts	Number of Questions	Time
Reading Comprehension	main idea, supporting idea, inferences, details, interpreting information	22	45 minutes
Writing	grammar, mechanics, paragraph logic and development	21	45 minutes
Mathematics	arithmetic, fractions and decimals, ratios and proportions, units and measurements	28	45 minutes
Science	body systems (muscular, skeletal, nervous, renal/urinary, endocrine, circulatory, and respiratory), electrolytes and homeostasis	20	30 minutes
Total		91 questions	2 hours and 45 minutes

How Is the Kaplan Nursing School Admissions Test Administered?

The Kaplan Nursing School Admissions Test is administered by individual health care education programs. Most programs will require you to create an account with Kaplan and to take the test at a specified testing location, usually on its campus. You should check with the program to which you are applying to find testing dates and locations. If you want to report your test score to a school at which you did not test, you will need to contact the school's admissions office.

Before you take the test, carefully check the policies and procedures for your test site. Fees and payment methods will vary by school. In addition, most schools will have specific requirements for what you will need to bring (e.g., identification, pencils) and what not to bring (e.g., calculators, cell phones).

The test will begin with a fifteen-minute tutorial that does not count toward the time limit for the exam.

Keep in mind that schools may require you to take the Kaplan Nursing Admissions Test the same year that you are applying.

How Is the Kaplan Nursing School Admissions Test Scored?

Scores are available immediately once you complete your exam. You may also access your scores through your Kaplan account.

You will receive a scaled percentage score ranging from 0 – 100 percent for each of the four sections of the exam and a cumulative percentage score reflecting your performance on the entire exam.

Minimum score requirements are determined by individual health care education programs. Check with your school to find out the minimum score required. Some schools require a cumulative score of 65 percent; others may require certain minimum scores on different sections.

Ascencia Test Prep

With health care fields such as nursing, pharmacy, emergency care, and physical therapy becoming the fastest-growing industries in the United States, individuals looking to enter the health care industry or rise in their field need high-quality, reliable resources. Ascencia Test Prep's study guides and test preparation materials are developed by credentialed industry professionals with years of experience in their respective fields. Ascencia recognizes that health care professionals nurture bodies and spirits, and save lives. Ascencia Test Prep's mission is to help health care workers grow.

ONE: READING

Reading Comprehension

On the KNAT, you must read nine short passages and answer twenty-two reading questions. You have forty-five minutes to complete this section.

Most passages will be about health or medicine. You do not need any outside knowledge to answer the questions.

Reading questions ask about reading comprehension skill: understanding the main idea of a passage, specific details, drawing inferences, and more. This section reviews different types of reading comprehension questions you will encounter.

THE MAIN IDEA

The **topic** is a word or short phrase that explains what a passage is about. The **main idea** is a complete sentence that explains what the author is trying to say about the topic. Generally, the **topic sentence** is the first (or near the first) sentence in a paragraph. It is a general statement that introduces the topic so that the reader knows what to expect.

The **summary sentence**, on the other hand, frequently (but not always!) comes at the end of a paragraph or passage because it wraps up all the ideas presented. This sentence summarizes what an author has said about the topic. Some passages, particularly short ones, will not include a summary sentence.

QUICK REVIEW

To find the main idea, identify the topic and then ask, "What is the author trying to tell me about the topic?"

Table 1.1. Identifying Topic and Main Idea

The cisco, a foot-long freshwater fish native to the Great Lakes, once thrived throughout the basin but had virtually disappeared by the 1950s. However, today fishermen are pulling them up by the net-load in Lake Michigan and Lake Ontario. It is highly unusual for a native species to revive, and the reason for the cisco's reemergence is even more unlikely. The cisco have an invasive species—quagga mussels—to thank for their return. Quagga mussels depleted nutrients in the lakes, harming other species highly dependent on these nutrients. Cisco, however, thrive in low-nutrient environments. As other species—many of which were invasive—diminished, cisco flourished in their place.

Table 1.1. Identifying Topic and Main Idea (continued)	
Topic sentence	The cisco, a foot-long freshwater fish native to the Great Lakes, once thrived throughout the basin but had virtually disappeared by the 1950s.
Topic	cisco
Summary sentence	As other species—many of which were invasive—diminished, cisco flourished in their place.
Main idea	Cisco had nearly disappeared from the lake, but now flourish thanks to the invasive quagga mussel.

PRACTICE QUESTIONS

1. Tourists flock to Yellowstone National Park each year to view the geysers that bubble and erupt throughout it. What most of these tourists do not know is that these geysers are formed by a caldera—a hot crater in the earth's crust—which was created by a series of three eruptions of an ancient super volcano. These eruptions, which began 2.1 million years ago, spewed between 1,000 to 2,450 cubic kilometers of volcanic matter at such a rate that the volcano's magma chamber collapsed, creating the craters.

    What is the topic of the passage?

    A) tourists

    B) geysers

    C) volcanic eruptions

    D) super volcanos

2. The Battle of Little Bighorn, commonly called Custer's Last Stand, was a battle between the Lakota, the Northern Cheyenne, the Arapaho, and the Seventh Cavalry Regiment of the US Army. Led by war leaders Crazy Horse and Chief Gall and the religious leader Sitting Bull, the allied tribes of the Plains Indians decisively defeated their US foes. Two hundred and sixty-eight US soldiers were killed, including General George Armstrong Custer, two of his brothers, his nephew, his brother-in-law, and six Indian scouts.

    What is the main idea of this passage?

    A) Most of General Custer's family died in the Battle of Little Bighorn.

    B) The Seventh Cavalry regiment was formed to fight Native American tribes.

    C) Sitting Bull and George Custer were fierce enemies.

    D) The Battle of Little Bighorn was a significant victory for the Plains Indians.

SUPPORTING DETAILS

Statements that describe or explain the main idea are **supporting details**. Supporting details are often found after the topic sentence. They support the main idea through examples, descriptions, and explanations.

HELPFUL HINT

To find supporting details, look for sentences that connect to the main idea and tell more about it.

Authors may add details to support their argument or claim. **Facts** are details that point to truths, while **opinions** are based on personal beliefs or judgments. To differentiate between fact and opinion, look for statements that express feelings, attitudes, or beliefs that can't be proven (opinions) and statements that can be proven (facts).

Table 1.2. Supporting Details and Fact and Opinion

Bait is an important element of fishing. Some people use live bait, such as worms and night crawlers. Others use artificial bait, such as lures and spinners. Live bait has a scent that fish are drawn to. Live bait is a good choice for fishing. It's cheap and easy to find. Lures can vibrate, make noise, and mimic the movements of some fish. People should choose artificial bait over live bait because it can be used multiple times.

Supporting details	Lures can vibrate, make noise, and mimic the movements of some fish.
Fact	Live bait has a scent that fish are drawn to.
Opinion	Live bait is a good choice for fishing.

PRACTICE QUESTIONS

3. Increasingly, companies are turning to subcontracting services rather than hiring full-time employees. This provides companies with advantages like greater flexibility, reduced legal responsibility to employees, and lower possibility of unionization within the company. However, this has led to increasing confusion and uncertainty over the legal definition of employment. Courts have grappled with questions about the hiring company's responsibility in maintaining fair labor practices. Companies argue that they delegate that authority to subcontractors, while unions and other worker advocate groups argue that companies still have a legal obligation to the workers who contribute to their business.

   Which detail BEST supports the idea that contracting employees is beneficial to companies?

   A) Uncertainty over the legal definition of employment increases.

   B) Companies still have a legal obligation to contractors.

   C) There is a lower possibility of unionization within the company.

   D) Contractors, not companies, control fair labor practices.

4. Chalk is a colorful way for kids and adults to have fun and be creative. Chalk is used on playgrounds and sidewalks. Children love to draw pictures in different colors. The designs are beautiful, but they are also messy. Chalk doesn't clean up easily. It has to wash away. Chalk is also used by cafés and bakeries. Shops use chalk to showcase their menus and special items. It is a great way to advertise their food.

   Which statement from the passage is an opinion?

   A) It is a great way to advertise their food.

   B) Chalk doesn't clean up easily.

   C) It has to wash away.

   D) Shops use chalk to showcase their menus and special items.

DRAWING CONCLUSIONS

Readers can use information that is **explicit**, or clearly stated, along with information that is **implicit**, or indirect, to make inferences and **draw conclusions**. Readers can determine meaning from what is implied by using details, context clues, and prior knowledge. When answering questions, consider what is known from personal

HELPFUL HINT

Look for facts, character actions and dialogue, how each sentence connects to the topic, and the author's reasoning for an argument when drawing conclusions.

experiences and make note of all information the author has provided before drawing a conclusion.

Table 1.3. Drawing Conclusions

When the Spanish-American War broke out in 1898, the US Army was small and under-staffed. President William McKinley called for 1,250 volunteers to serve in the First US Volunteer Calvary. The ranks were quickly filled by cowboys, gold prospectors, hunters, gamblers, Native Americans, veterans, police officers, and college students looking for an adventure. The officer corps was composed of veterans of previous wars. With more volunteers than it could accept, the army set high standards: all the recruits had to be skilled on horseback and with guns. Consequently, they became known as the Rough Riders.

Question	Why are the volunteers named Rough Riders?
Explicit information	different people volunteered, men were looking for adventure, recruits had to be extremely skilled on horseback and with guns due to a glut of volunteers
Implicit information	Men had previous occupations, officer corps veterans worked with volunteers.
Conclusion drawn	The men were called Rough Riders because they were inexperienced yet particularly enthusiastic to help with the war and were willing to put in extra effort to join.

PRACTICE QUESTION

5. After World War I, political and social forces pushed for a return to normalcy in the United States. The result was disengagement from the larger world and increased focus on American economic growth and personal enjoyment. Caught in the middle were American writers, raised on the values of the prewar world and frustrated with what they viewed as the superficiality and materialism of postwar American culture. Many of them fled to Paris, where they became known as the "lost generation," creating a trove of literary works criticizing their home culture and delving into their own feelings of alienation.

Which conclusion about the effects of war is most likely true?

A) War served as an inspiration for literary works.

B) It was difficult to stabilize countries after war occurred.

C) Writers were torn between supporting war and their own ideals.

D) Individual responsibility and global awareness declined after the war.

THE AUTHOR'S PURPOSE AND POINT OF VIEW

The **author's purpose** is an author's reason for writing a text. Authors may write to share an experience, entertain, persuade, or inform readers. This can be done through persuasive, expository, and narrative writing.

Persuasive writing influences the actions and thoughts of readers. Authors state an opinion, then provide reasons that support the opinion. **Expository writing** outlines and explains steps in a process. Authors focus on a sequence of events. **Narrative writing** tells a story. Authors include a setting, plot, characters, problem, and solution in the text.

Authors also share their **point of view** (perspectives, attitudes, and beliefs) with readers. Identify the author's point of view by word choice, details, descriptions, and characters' actions. The author's attitude or **tone** can be found in word choice that conveys feelings or stance on a topic.

Text structure is the way the author organizes a text. A text can be organized to show problem and solution, comparison and contrast, or even cause and effect. Structure of a text can give insight into an author's purpose and point of view. If a text is organized to pose an argument or advertise a product, it can be considered persuasive. The author's point of view will be revealed in how thoughts and opinions are expressed in the text.

STUDY TIP
Use the acronym **P.I.E.S.**—*persuade*, *inform*, *entertain*, *state*—to help you remember elements of an author's purpose.

Table 1.4. The Author's Purpose and Point of View

Superfoods are foods that are found in nature. They contain rich nutrients and are low in calories. Many people are concerned about healthy diets and weight loss, so superfoods are a great meal choice! Rich antioxidants and vitamins found in superfoods decrease the risk of diseases and aid in heart health.

Author's purpose	persuade readers of the benefit of superfoods
Point of view	advocates superfoods as "a great meal choice"
Tone	positive, encouraging, pointing out the benefits of superfoods, using positive words like *great* and *rich*
Structure	cause and effect to show use of superfoods and results

PRACTICE QUESTIONS

6. University of California, Berkeley, researchers decided to tackle an age-old problem: why shoelaces come untied. They recorded the shoelaces of a volunteer walking on a treadmill by attaching devices to record the acceleration, or g-force, experienced by the knot. The results were surprising. A shoelace knot experiences more g-force from a person walking than any rollercoaster can generate. However, if the person simply stomped or swung their feet—the two movements that make up a walker's stride—the g-force was not enough to undo the knots.

What is the purpose of this passage?

A) to confirm if shoelaces always come undone

B) to compare the force of treadmills and rollercoasters

C) to persuade readers to tie their shoes tighter

D) to describe the results of an experiment on shoelaces

7. What do you do with plastic bottles? Do you throw them away, or do you recycle or reuse them? As landfills continue to fill up, there will eventually be no place to put our trash. If you recycle or reuse bottles, you will help reduce waste and turn something old into a creative masterpiece!

Which of the following BEST describes what the author believes?

A) Landfills are unnecessary.

B) Reusing objects requires creativity.

C) Recycling helps the environment.

D) Reusing objects is better than recycling.

8. Negative cinematic representations of gorillas have provoked fear and contribute to hunting practices that endanger gorilla populations. It's a shame that many films portray them as scary and aggressive creatures. Their size and features should not be cause for alarm. Gorillas are actually shy and act aggressively only when provoked.

What can be inferred about the author's attitude toward gorillas?

A) The author is surprised that people do not know the truth about gorillas.

B) The author is concerned that movies distort people's opinion of gorillas.

C) The author is saddened by the decrease in gorilla populations.

D) The author is afraid that gorillas are being provoked.

9. Want smoother skin? Try *Face Lace*, a mix of shea butter and coconut oil. Like most creams, it's soft and easy to apply. We rank #1 in sales and free trials. Our competitor *Smooth Moves* may be great for blemishes, but we excel at reducing the signs of aging!

What is the structure of this text?

A) cause and effect

B) order and sequence

C) problem and solution

D) compare and contrast

COMPARING PASSAGES

Sometimes readers need to compare and contrast two texts. After reading and identifying the main idea of each text, look for similarities and differences in the main idea, details, claims, evidence, characters, and so on.

When answering questions about two texts, first identify whether the question is about a similarity or a difference. Then look for specific details in the text that connect to the answers. After that, determine which answer choice best describes the similarity or difference.

HELPFUL HINT

Use a Venn diagram, table, or highlighters to organize similarities and differences between texts.

Table 1.5. Comparing Passages

Apple Cider Vinegar

Apple cider vinegar has many medicinal properties. It is used for cleaning and disinfecting. When ingested, it lowers blood sugar levels, increasing insulin function and fighting diabetes. Studies are being conducted to determine if it can aid in shrinking tumors and cancer cells, and lower the risk of heart disease.

Alkaline Water

Many people believe that alkaline water increases immune system support; prevents cancer; and aids in antiaging, detoxification, and weight loss. Unfortunately, having an excess amount of alkaline water in the body could produce nausea, vomiting, and tremors.

Similarities (comparison)	Both substances are ingested and used to fight diseases.
Differences (contrast)	Alkaline water has negative side effects, whereas apple cider vinegar is being studied to prove its usefulness.

PRACTICE QUESTION

10. Panda Bears

Panda bears live in China's bamboo forests. They eat bamboo and are excellent tree climbers. New roads and railroads break the flow of the forest, isolating panda populations. This decreases the amount of food pandas can access during the year.

Polar Bears

Polar bears live in the Arctic and are the largest land carnivores in the world. They eat seals and walruses. As the sea gets larger from melting ice, polar bears have to travel longer distances for food. Their thick white fur provides warmth and traction for their feet on the ice. They are good swimmers.

Which of these statements BEST compares the information in both texts?

A) A carnivore's diet depends on animals in the area.

B) The destruction of habitats affects food supply.

C) Animals must be able to move easily in their environment.

D) An animal's population can change its habitat.

MEANING OF WORDS

To understand the meanings of unfamiliar words, use **context clues**. Context clues are hints the author provides to help readers define difficult words. They can be found in words or phrases in the same sentence or in a neighboring sentence. Look for synonyms, antonyms, definitions, examples, and explanations in the text to determine the meaning of the unfamiliar word.

Sometimes parts of a word can make its meaning easier to determine. **Affixes** are added to **root words** (a word's basic form) to modify meaning. **Prefixes** are added to the beginning of root words, while **suffixes** are added to the ending. Divide words into parts, finding meaning in each part. Take, for example, the word *unjustifiable*: the prefix is *un–* (*not*), the root word is *justify* ("to prove reasonable"), and the suffix is *–able* (referring to a quality).

Another way to determine the meaning of unknown words is to consider their denotation and connotation with other words in the sentence. **Denotation** is the literal meaning of a word, while **connotation** is the positive or negative associations of a word.

Authors use words to convey thoughts, but the meaning may be different from a literal meaning of the words. This is called **figurative language**. Types of figurative language include similes, metaphors, hyperboles, and personification.

Similes compare two things that are not alike with the words *like* or *as*. Metaphors are used to compare two things that are not exactly alike but may share a certain characteristic.

Hyperboles are statements that exaggerate something in order to make a point or draw attention to a certain feature. Personification involves using human characteristics to describe an animal or object.

HELPFUL HINT

Use what you know about a word to figure out its meaning, then look for clues in the sentence or paragraph.

Table 1.6. Meanings of Words	
Have you ever gone to a flea market? There are rows of furniture, clothing, and antiques waiting for discovery. Unlike a museum with items on display, flea markets are opportunities to learn and shop. Vendors bring their handmade goods to this communal event to show their crafts and make money.	
Context clues	Vendors are people who sell things; people shop at a flea market.
Affixes	The prefix com– in communal means with or together.
Meaning	Communal means "shared with a community."

PRACTICE QUESTIONS

11. The Bastille, Paris's famous historical prison, was originally built in 1370 as a fortification—called a *bastide* in Old French—to protect the city from English invasion. It rose 100 feet into the air, had eight towers, and was surrounded by a moat more than eighty feet wide. In the seventeenth century, the government **converted** the fortress into an elite prison for upper-class felons, political disruptors, and spies.

    Which word or phrase can be used to determine the meaning of *converted*?

    A) originally built

    B) fortification

    C) felons

    D) historical prison

12. Breaking a world record is no easy feat. An application and video submission of an amazing skill may not be enough. Potential record breakers may need to demonstrate their skill in front of an official world records judge. The judge will watch a performance of a record attempt to determine if the record-breaking claim is **credible**. After all evidence is collected, reviewed, and approved, a certificate for the new world record is granted!

    Based on affixes and context clues, what does *credible* mean?

    A) believable

    B) achievable

    C) likeable

    D) noticeable

13. Every year people gather in Durham Park to participate in the Food Truck Rodeo. A band plays, and the food trucks are like a carnival of delicious treats. The aroma of food draws all who pass by, creating a large crowd. The event is free to attend; patrons pay only for what they want to eat. From pizzas and burgers to hotdogs and pastries, there's something for everyone!

    Which type of figurative language is used in the second sentence?

    A) hyperbole

    B) metaphor

    C) personification

    D) simile

RECOGNIZING SEQUENCES

Signal words indicate steps of a process, reveal a sequence of events, or show the **logic** of a passage. These words will tell you when things need to happen in a certain order. Signal words should show a transition from one event or step to another.

When reading a passage, you will find that signal words can be used to follow the direction of the author's ideas and the sequence of events. Signal words show time order and how details flow in a chronological way.

HELPFUL HINT

To find signal words, ask, "What happened first and what happened after that?"

Table 1.7. Following Directions and Recognizing Sequences

NASA wanted to launch a man from Earth to the moon. At first they used satellites for launch tests. Then in June of 1968, astronauts aboard the Apollo 8 launched into space and circled the moon ten times before returning to Earth. Finally, in 1969 three astronauts reached the moon in the Apollo 11 spacecraft. After a successful landing, two members of the crew walked on the moon. During their walk they collected data and samples of rocks. They returned as heroes of space exploration.	
Signal words	At first, then, finally, after, during

PRACTICE QUESTION

14. Babies learn to move their bodies over time. Head control is first developed at two months to create strong neck, back, and tummy muscles. Next, the abilities to reach, grasp, and sit up with support happen around four to six months. By the end of six months, babies learn to roll over. After six to nine months, babies can sit on their own and crawl. During age nine to twelve months, pulling and standing up are mastered. Finally, after gaining good balance, babies take their first steps!

    Which BEST describes the order of a baby's movement over time?

    A) roll over, control head, sit up, crawl

    B) sit up, roll over, crawl, walk

    C) control head, reach, crawl, roll over

    D) sit up, grasp, crawl, walk

Reading Review Questions

Chronic traumatic encephalopathy (CTE) is a degenerative brain disease that has garnered the attention of the media in recent years. Medical studies have indicated that American football players have a higher chance of developing CTE than many other athletes because of the repeated brain trauma that results from helmet-to-helmet collisions on the field. Some studies have found that nearly 87 percent of all football players show signs of CTE. This is a troubling statistic, considering that CTE has been linked to memory loss, mood disorders, and even dementia. There is also a strong correlation with CTE and suicide, and it may be the high percentage of suicides among former NFL players that has shed light on the troubling symptoms of chronic head trauma.

Many organizations, colleges, and high schools have responded by introducing stricter standards for concussion protocols and head-to-head collisions. However, even these protocols have done little to mitigate the traumatic consequences of accidental helmet-to-helmet collisions that occur on a daily basis on football fields across the country. Many concerned parents have begun to ask if football is too violent a sport for their children. It may be too early for Americans to honestly answer this question, but there is certainly room for growing concern. Recent statistics show a decline in enrollment in youth football programs across the country, and for good reason: head trauma—no matter how many times or how often—appears to have long-term effects on the brain and the mind.

1. Which sentence best summarizes the passage's main idea?

   A) CTE is a degenerative brain disease that a large percentage of American football players develop.

   B) CTE has been linked to memory loss, mood disorders, dementia, and suicide among former NFL players.

   C) Many organizations, colleges, and high schools have introduced stricter standards for concussion protocols and head-to-head collisions.

   D) Stricter protocols have done little to alleviate the results of accidental helmet-to-helmet collisions that occur on football fields.

2. What is the meaning of the word *garnered* in the first sentence?

   A) harvested

   B) gotten

   C) stored

   D) accumulated

3. Which of the following is NOT listed as a detail in the passage?

   A) Studies have shown that American football players have a higher chance of developing CTE than other athletes do.

   B) When playing football, players sustain repeated brain trauma from helmet-to-helmet collisions.

   C) Studies have shown that nearly 87 percent of all football players show signs of CTE.

   D) Professional football organizations across the United States are taking responsibility for the high incidence of CTE among players.

4. What is the author's primary purpose in writing this essay?

   A) to reassure readers that football players' brains can heal from CTE

   B) to suggest that, following any kind of head trauma, an athlete should take several months off to heal

   C) to suggest that football may be too violent a sport for children and teenagers to play

   D) to persuade readers not to allow their children to play high school sports such as football

5. Readers can infer from reading this passage that professional football's future _____.

   A) may be threatened

   B) will not be affected by CTE studies

   C) will definitely be threatened

   D) should be threatened, due to suicides among former players

6. In the second paragraph, the author writes, "It may be too early for Americans to honestly answer this question, but there is certainly room for growing concern." To which question does the author refer?

   A) Is playing professional football worth suffering memory loss, mood disorders, and dementia?

   B) Should football fans stop attending games and watching football on television?

   C) Is CTE so painful that it causes sufferers to commit suicide?

   D) Is tackle football too violent a sport for children?

Have you ever wondered why exactly we feel pain when we get hurt? Or why some patients feel phantom pain even in the absence of a real trauma or damage? Pain is a highly sophisticated biological mechanism, one that is often downplayed or misinterpreted. Pain is much more than a measure of tissue damage—it is a complex neurological chain reaction that sends sensory data to the brain. Pain is not produced by the toe you stubbed; rather, it is produced once the information about the "painful" incident reaches the brain. The brain analyzes the sensory signals emanating from the toe you stubbed, but the toe itself is not producing the sensation of pain.

In most cases, the brain offers accurate interpretations of the sensory data that is sent to it via the neurological processes in the body. If you hold your hand too close to a fire, for instance, the brain triggers pain that causes you to jerk your hand away, preventing further damage.

Phantom pain, most commonly associated with the amputation or loss of a limb, on the other hand, is triggered even in the absence of any injury. One possible explanation is that the spinal cord is still processing sensations from that area.

The science of pain management is complex and still poorly understood. However, anesthetics or anti-inflammatory medications can reduce or relieve pain by disrupting the neurological pathways that produce it. The absence of pain, however, is a double-edged sword—sometimes pain is the only clue to an underlying injury or disease. Likewise, an injury or disease can dull or eliminate pain, making it impossible to sense when something is actually wrong.

7. Readers can infer from the passage that pain is _____.

    A) simple: pain is painful

    B) more complicated than most people know

    C) caused by the body's system of endocrine glands

    D) often exaggerated in patients' minds

8. What does the term "phantom pain" mean in the first and third paragraphs?

    A) ghostly pain

    B) pain that is *not* the result of an injury

    C) mild pain

    D) pain that is "a double-edged sword"

9. Which sentence best summarizes the passage's main idea?

    A) Many people wonder why we feel pain when we are injured, or why some patients feel phantom pain.

    B) Pain is a complicated biological process, one that many people misjudge or do not understand.

    C) When you stub your toe, your brain analyzes the sensory signals coming from your injury.

    D) Anti-inflammatory medications can lessen or ease pain by affecting neurological processes.

10. According to the passage, what is true of phantom pain?

    A) It is psychological, not physical; in other words, it is not real.

    B) Biologists are mystified by this kind of pain.

    C) It occurs because the body remembers how painful it felt when a limb was severely injured.

    D) It may happen because the spinal cord is still processing sensations from an amputated limb.

11. On which system of the human body does the author focus in this passage?

    A) the neurological system

    B) the immune system

    C) the circulatory system

    D) the cardiovascular system

12. In the last paragraph, the phrase "a double-edged sword" means that the absence of pain can be _____.

   A) positive or negative

   B) mild or unbearable

   C) caused by knife wounds

   D) even more painful than pain

In the digital age, with all its technological advances, it is hard to imagine a world without modern medical breakthroughs. But what we now consider "modern" medicine is still a relatively new phenomenon, having truly begun to develop in the nineteenth century. Many historians look to the scientific and technological advancements that followed the Industrial Revolution in the late eighteenth century and the Civil War in the nineteenth century as the beginnings of modern medicine.

Before the 1840s, surgery did not include the use of anesthesia. But on October 16, 1846, the first public demonstration of using ether to render a patient unconscious and immune to pain during surgery made waves throughout the medical community. Before the discovery of anesthesia, patients had to merely endure as doctors sliced into their bodies with scalpels. The types of surgeries that could be performed remained limited because it was nearly impossible to carry out more advanced operations or research while patients were writhing in pain.

Just twenty years later, the unprecedented bloodshed of the Civil War resulted in many medical innovations. Although many of the battlefield practices seem barbaric by today's standards, the sheer volume of medical need encouraged medical personnel, public health advocates, scientists, and inventors to seek more effective and humane treatment. Advances in amputation techniques, infection control, and transport of patients all stem from Civil War medicine. In addition, plastic surgery and prosthetics design took turns for the better after the war. As a result, the late nineteenth and early twentieth centuries witnessed a wave of new medicines, tools, and technologies.

13. Which of the following statements can the reader infer from the passage?

   A) During the Civil War, army doctors performed so many surgeries that they often ran out of ether.

   B) After the Civil War there was a shortage of men, so United States medical schools began accepting women.

   C) During the Civil War there was little money available to buy ether, and surgeons stopped using it for a few years.

   D) Years after the Civil War was over, surgical patients benefitted from the sheer number of surgeries army doctors performed during the war.

14. What is the author's primary purpose in writing this passage?

    A) to inform readers about the latest breakthroughs in surgical techniques

    B) to give a history of modern medicine from the 1840s through the early 1900s

    C) to inform readers about "barbaric" medical practices that occurred in army hospitals during the Civil War

    D) to convince readers that the Civil War was mainly good for the United States, even though many thousands died

15. Which sentence best summarizes the passage's main idea?

    A) "In the digital age ... it is hard to imagine a world without modern medical breakthroughs."

    B) "The scientific and technological advancements that followed the Industrial Revolution in the late eighteenth century and the Civil War in the nineteenth century [were] the beginnings of modern medicine."

    C) "On October 16, 1846, the first public demonstration of using ether to render a patient unconscious and immune to pain during surgery made waves throughout the medical community."

    D) "The unprecedented bloodshed of the Civil War resulted in many medical innovations."

16. The author writes that "plastic surgery and prosthetics design took turns for the better" after the Civil War ended. Readers can infer that this occurred because so many soldiers _____ as a result of the war.

    A) suffered post-traumatic stress disorder

    B) dreamed of going to medical school

    C) died of injuries and diseases

    D) lost limbs and were disfigured

17. According to the passage, how did the Civil War affect modern medicine?

    A) The war caused advancements in medicine to cease for a few years.

    B) The war did not greatly affect modern medicine.

    C) The war caused advancements in many branches of medicine.

    D) The war encouraged surgeons to use ether as an anesthetic.

18. In the second paragraph, what does the word *endure* mean?

    A) bear the pain

    B) brave the hardships

    C) survive the shortages

    D) continue living

Aside from the uterus itself, the placenta is, perhaps, the most important organ directly involved with pregnancy. It is an organ that only exists during pregnancy; it is delivered after birth. Connected to the fetus through the umbilical cord, the placenta is a nutrient-rich organ attached to the wall of the uterus. It not only nourishes the fetus with crucial gases (i.e., oxygen), but it also protects the fetus by carrying away wastes.

Some scientists describe the placenta as a kind of "trading post." It exchanges nutrients between the blood supplies of the mother and the fetus—although the blood supplies do not intermingle throughout this process. Nutrients from the fetal blood and maternal blood are instead exchanged and regulated via blood vessels that filter each source without bringing them in direct contact. Since the maternal blood delivers nutrients to the fetus, pregnant people should strive for a healthy lifestyle. Certain substances can pass through the placenta, causing problems for the developing fetus. Alcohol, tobacco, and drugs are among the products that can cause lifelong medical complications or disorders.

19. Which sentence best summarizes the passage's main idea?

   A) "Aside from the uterus itself, the placenta is, perhaps, the most important organ directly involved with pregnancy."

   B) "Some scientists describe the placenta as a kind of 'trading post.'"

   C) "Nutrients from the fetal blood and maternal blood are instead exchanged and regulated via blood vessels that filter each source without bringing them in direct contact."

   D) "Alcohol, tobacco, and drugs are among the products that can cause lifelong medical complications or disorders."

20. What is the meaning of the word *intermingle* in the second paragraph?

   A) intermix

   B) interact

   C) amalgamate

   D) fuse

21. Which of the following is NOT listed as a detail in the passage?

   A) The placenta is delivered after the baby is born.

   B) The placenta is attached to the uterine wall.

   C) Some scientists call the placenta a "trading post."

   D) The placenta protects the fetus from alcohol, tobacco, and drugs.

22. What is the author's primary purpose in writing this essay?

   A) to persuade pregnant women to avoid alcohol, tobacco, and drugs

   B) to inform readers about the placenta functions during pregnancy

   C) to explain the "trading post" metaphor that some scientists use

   D) to advise women to have their placentas checked regularly

23. Readers can infer from reading this passage that during pregnancy, the placenta is second in importance to the _____.

   A) mother

   B) fetus

   C) uterus

   D) blood

24. In the last sentence the author writes, "Alcohol, tobacco, and drugs are among the products that can cause lifelong medical complications or disorders." For whom or what can these substances cause "lifelong complications or disorders"?

   A) the uterus

   B) the placenta

   C) the mother

   D) the baby

A devastating condition known as microcephaly has been affecting newborn babies across the world. Microcephaly literally means "small head." It can occur when a fetus's brain stops developing in utero. There is no known cure, and many babies born with microcephaly have other problems as a result, such as developmental delays or loss of hearing or vision. This microcephaly epidemic is strongly correlated with the mosquito-borne disease known as the Zika virus. As government authorities look to resolve this public health risk, scientists are working hard in their laboratories to better understand the connection between the Zika virus and microcephaly.

Thus far, evidence has shown that if a mother contracts Zika, either by being bitten by an infected mosquito or engaging in sexual activity with someone infected, the virus has the ability to cross the placental barrier between the mother and fetus. While Zika causes only mild symptoms—or more commonly, none—in the mother, it has more detrimental effects on the developing fetus. While researchers are rushing to find a cure or a vaccine, health officials are worried that the Zika virus might eventually mutate, making a cure even more elusive. Americans who are pregnant or planning to become pregnant have been advised not to travel to areas where Zika is known to be present, or if they must, to take great care to avoid mosquito bites.

25. Which sentence best summarizes the passage's main idea?

   A) Microcephaly, a terrible condition that affects newborns, is caused by the Zika virus.

   B) Public health authorities are trying to resolve the microcephaly epidemic.

   C) Research scientists are striving to better understand the link between the Zika virus and microcephaly.

   D) The Zika virus causes only mild symptoms in the mother, but it stops her baby's brain from developing properly.

26. What is the meaning of the word *devastating* in the first sentence?

    A) demolishing

    B) very harmful

    C) confounding

    D) very disturbing

27. Which of the following is NOT listed as a detail in the passage?

    A) The word *microcephaly* means "small head."

    B) Microcephaly causes a fetus's brain to stop developing.

    C) Babies born with microcephaly may have developmental delays, hearing loss, or blindness.

    D) The Zika virus has been reported in northwest India.

28. What is the author's primary purpose in writing this essay?

    A) to reassure readers that there are no cases of microcephaly in the continental United States

    B) to inform readers about the link between the mosquito-borne Zika virus and microcephaly

    C) to persuade pregnant women to avoid traveling to areas where there are mosquitoes

    D) to advise readers on ways to treat pregnant women who have been exposed to Zika virus

29. Readers can infer from reading this passage that scientists have not yet _____.

    A) learned that a mother who contracts Zika virus may give birth to a child with microcephaly

    B) proven that the Zika virus is mosquito borne

    C) studied case histories of patients who gave birth to babies with microcephaly

    D) discovered everything they want to know about the link between Zika virus and microcephaly

30. In the hyphenated word *mosquito-borne*, what does the word *borne* mean?

    A) tolerated

    B) accepted

    C) exhibited

    D) carried

Recent reports by the World Health Organization's International Agency for Research on Cancer claim that certain chemicals used to cure meats may increase your chance of getting cancer. In particular, the studies claim that nitrates used to preserve and flavor processed foods such as hot dogs, bacon, beef jerky, sausages, cold cuts, and smoked meats may be one of the leading causes of the recent spike in cancer rates in developed countries. Nitrates have been specifically connected to two common types of cancer: colon cancer and stomach cancer.

Grilling and smoking these processed meats may produce even more cancer-causing compounds. These new findings have been downplayed by many American and European meat industries and lobbying groups. Meat producers across the globe are disputing the claims, saying that they are unfounded. But health agencies such as the American Cancer Society are applauding the research, claiming that it reinforces what they have known for years: processed meats are problematic for your health. Nevertheless, until more research emerges, the debate will wage on over the legitimacy of the risks associated with eating processed meats such as salami and sausage. On one side, health organizations are saying take it easy on the hot dogs; on the other side, the meat industry is claiming it's all just baloney.

31. From reading the second paragraph, readers can infer that the author is trying to _____ us.

    A) inform and persuade

    B) inform and entertain

    C) warn and persuade

    D) amuse and entertain

32. Why does the author use the word *baloney* in the last sentence?

    A) because baloney is not a processed meat product

    B) to show that lunch meats contain nitrates

    C) to create a play on words: *baloney* is slang for "nonsense"

    D) to rhyme with the words *macaroni* and *pony*

33. Which sentence best summarizes the passage's main idea?

    A) Most meats cause cancer, even though the meat industry claims this is "baloney."

    B) Health groups have done studies that show some processed meats cause cancer.

    C) Grilling and smoking cured meats such as hotdogs makes them even more carcinogenic.

    D) Nitrates—which are used to cure meats—have been linked to colon cancer and stomach cancer.

34. Using information from the passage, which can readers infer might be MOST carcinogenic?

   A) roast beef that is not cured

   B) fried chicken that is neither smoked nor barbequed

   C) hotdogs grilled on a barbecue over charcoal briquets

   D) bacon fried in a pan with eggs sunny-side up

35. In the last sentence, what does the phrase "take it easy on" mean?

   A) don't criticize so harshly

   B) don't take everything so seriously

   C) don't use such fancy language

   D) don't eat very many

Sugar is an essential fuel for the human body. However, Americans, on average, are consuming twenty *more* teaspoons of sugar daily than the American Heart Association's recommendation of six teaspoons for women and nine for men. The reason for this excess is twofold: humans may have an evolutionary hunger for sugar, and food companies are capitalizing on this human sweet tooth. As a result, millions of Americans are suffering from obesity, diabetes, and tooth decay.

When the body breaks down food, it only uses some simple sugars for immediate energy; the rest of the sugar is stored as fat that can be called upon for energy later. The issue is that millions of people are storing too much fat because they are simply eating too much sugar. In addition to its obvious sources—cake, cookies, soda—added sugar lurks in many supposedly healthy foods, such as tomato sauce, yogurt, granola, and fruit snacks. In particular, low-fat versions of some of these foods are packed with extra sugar to improve the flavor lost by reducing the fat content.

Foods that naturally contain sugar offer a healthy alternative to processed foods with added sugar. The naturally occurring sugar in fruits and vegetables is accompanied by fiber and other nutritional elements. That is why health professionals recommend that children trade in their cans of soda for a handful of grapes or a plate of sweet potatoes. These so-called smart sweets help Americans satiate their sugar fix while also giving them the appropriate fuel to enjoy a healthy life.

36. What is the main idea of the passage?

   A) Sugar provides fuel for the human body.

   B) Consuming too much sugar causes obesity, diabetes, and tooth decay.

   C) Americans are eating too much sugar, experts say.

   D) Foods such as tomato sauce, yogurt, and granola contain added sugar.

37. What is the meaning of the word *fuel* in the first sentence?

    A) energy source

    B) gas or gasoline

    C) petroleum

    D) stimulate

38. Which of the following is NOT listed as a detail in the passage?

    A) The American Heart Association recommends that women consume only six teaspoons of sugar per day.

    B) Human beings may have evolved to crave sugar.

    C) Some sugar is stored as fat; the body can use fat for energy at a later time.

    D) Corn syrup, an ingredient in some foods, contains a great deal of sugar.

39. What is the author's primary purpose in writing this essay?

    A) to inform readers about Americans' overconsumption of sugar

    B) to warn patients that they are in grave danger of becoming obese or diabetic

    C) to criticize the food industry for cynically taking advantage of Americans' sugar addiction

    D) to reassure Americans that a little more sugar than the recommended amount is usually OK

40. Which of the following statements can readers infer from the passage?

    A) If you are a man and you consume ten teaspoons of sugar per day, you are certainly endangering your health.

    B) If you are a woman and you consume twenty-six teaspoons of sugar per day, you are likely to be—or to become—overweight.

    C) If you are a child and you drink one sugary soda drink per day, you are sure to have tooth decay.

    D) Homo sapiens living in prehistoric times were unable to find enough sugar to fuel their bodies.

Biotechnology has been revolutionizing the medical profession for decades. Pills that can transmit medical data and smartphones that can monitor asthma symptoms are among the advances being made. Now biotechnologists are taking aim at one of the most fear-inducing medical instruments in history: the hypodermic syringe needle.

The hypodermic syringe needle has been sticking patients since the 1850s, but the creation of a new, transdermal vaccine delivery system may make the needle obsolete. This new device is a pain-free vaccination tool that does not need refrigeration like some vaccines delivered via syringe. The tiny patch, which is smaller than a postage stamp, latches on to human skin via a spring-loading mechanism. The patch injects medications into the body's cells without injuring patients like hypodermic needles do. It has thousands of tiny needles—just microns in diameter—coated in the vaccine that pierce only the top layer of the skin. This causes no pain, does not require special training to deliver, and should alleviate the fear felt by the needle-phobic. Scientists believe transdermal vaccines may be able to supplant hypodermic needles for medical practitioners carrying out vaccination efforts in developing nations. While diseases like polio have been eradicated in the United States, they still affect populations in developing nations. This new technology could change the lives of millions of people around the globe.

41. Which of the following statements can the reader infer from the passage?

   A) The tiny patch is a cheaper vaccine delivery system than the hypodermic syringe needle.

   B) The hypodermic syringe needle is a cheaper vaccine delivery system than the tiny patch.

   C) The tiny patch is a more convenient vaccine delivery system than the hypodermic syringe needle.

   D) The hypodermic syringe needle is a more convenient vaccine delivery system than the tiny patch.

42. What is the author's primary purpose in writing this passage?

   A) to advise readers on ways to vaccinate patients around the globe

   B) to warn readers that hypodermic syringe needles can scare patients

   C) to tell readers some exciting news about a pain-free vaccination tool

   D) to tell a story about a doctor who travels the world vaccinating people

43. Which sentence best summarizes the passage's main idea?

   A) "Biotechnology has been revolutionizing the medical profession for decades."

   B) "Pills that can transmit medical data and smartphones that can monitor asthma symptoms are among the advances being made."

   C) "The hypodermic syringe needle has been sticking patients since the 1850s, but the creation of a new, transdermal vaccine delivery system may make the needle obsolete."

   D) "It has thousands of tiny needles—just microns in diameter—coated in the vaccine that pierce only the top layer of the skin."

44. In the second paragraph, what does the word part *dermal* in the word *transdermal* most likely mean?

   A) data

   B) fear

   C) needle

   D) skin

45. According to the passage, how might the invention of transdermal vaccines affect people around the globe?

A) by eradicating diseases more quickly and efficiently

B) by making the vaccination process pleasurable rather than painful

C) by doubling the cost of vaccines used by world health professionals

D) by encouraging young people to enter the biotechnology field

46. In the second paragraph, what does the word *supplant* mean?

A) improve

B) replace

C) outlaw

D) buy

1.   **B) is correct.** The topic of the passage is geysers. Tourists, volcanic eruptions, and super volcanos are all mentioned in the explanation of what geysers are and how they are formed.

2.   **D) is correct.** The author writes that "the allied tribes…decisively defeated their US foes," and the remainder of the passage provides details to support this idea.

3.   **C) is correct.** The passage specifically presents this detail as one of the advantages of subcontracting services.

4.   **A) is correct.** The statement "It is a great way to advertise their food" is a judgment about how the shops use chalk to show menu items to customers. The word *great* expresses a feeling, and the idea cannot be proven.

5.   **D) is correct.** After the war, there was a lack of focus on the world and greater focus on personal comforts, which writers viewed as superficiality and materialism.

6.   **D) is correct.** The text provides details on the experiment as well as its results.

7.   **C) is correct.** The author states that recycling and reusing objects reduces waste, which helps the environment.

8.   **B) is correct.** The author demonstrates disapproval of film portrayals of gorillas and how they influence people's views of gorillas.

9.   **D) is correct.** In this text, two brands of cream are being compared and contrasted.

10. **B) is correct.** Both passages indicate that habitats are diminishing, impacting access to food.

11. **A) is correct.** *Fortification* and *fortress* are synonyms. In the seventeenth century, the purpose of the fortress changed. This is a clue that *converted* means "a change in form or function."

12. **A) is correct.** The root *cred* means *believe*. The words *evidence, reviewed,* and *approved* are context clues hinting that something needs to be believed and accepted.

13. **D) is correct.** The author compares the food trucks to "a carnival of delicious treats," using the word *like*.

14. **B) is correct.** According to the passage, a baby achieves milestones in independent movement in this order. Use the ages and signal words to determine the order of events.

1.   **A) is correct.** The passage is mainly about the large number of American football players who develop CTE. The other sentences give details from the passage.

2.   **B) is correct.** In the first sentence, the author writes, "Chronic traumatic encephalopathy (CTE) is a degenerative brain disease that has garnered the attention of the media in recent years." The context shows that the author uses the phrase "garnered the attention of the media" to mean "gotten the attention of the news media."

3.   **D) is correct.** The passage does not contain this detail. The passage does not mention what stance professional football organizations are taking regarding CTE.

4.   **C) is correct.** In the first paragraph, the author points out that studies have shown that the vast majority of professional football players develop CTE, a serious brain illness. The second paragraph deals primarily with implications for younger athletes. The author writes, "Many concerned parents have begun to ask if football is too violent a sport for their children." The evidence in the passage suggests that the author may think that football is too violent for athletes of all ages.

5.   **A) is correct.** The author does not say whether studies on CTE among players have affected professional football one way or another. However, readers can infer that professional football's success may be threatened in the future, depending on public reaction to the studies.

6.   **D) is correct.** In the second paragraph, the author writes, "Many concerned parents have begun to ask if football is too violent a sport for their children. It may be too early for Americans to honestly answer this question, but there is certainly room for growing concern."

7.   **B) is correct.** In the first paragraph, the author writes, "Pain is a highly sophisticated biological mechanism, one that is often downplayed or misinterpreted. Pain is much more than a measure of tissue damage—it is a complex neurological chain reaction that sends sensory data to the brain."

8.   **B) is correct.** In the third paragraph, the author writes, "Phantom pain, most commonly associated with the amputation or loss of a limb, ... is triggered even in the absence of any injury. One possible explanation is that the spinal cord is still processing sensations from that area."

9.   **B) is correct.** The passage is mainly about the fact that pain is a complicated process. The other sentences provide details from the passage.

10. **D) is correct.** In paragraph 3, the author writes, "Phantom pain [may be caused when] the spinal cord [continues to process] sensations from that area."

11. **A) is correct.** In the first paragraph, the author writes, "Pain ... is a complex neurological chain reaction that sends sensory data to the brain."

12. **A) is correct.** In the last paragraph, the author writes, "The absence of pain ... is a double-edged sword—sometimes pain is the only clue to an underlying injury or disease. Likewise, an injury or disease can dull or eliminate pain, making it impossible to sense when something is actually wrong." Readers can infer that the author is using

the metaphor of a double-edged sword to show that the absence of pain is not always positive.

13. **D) is correct.** In the third paragraph, the author writes, "The sheer volume of medical need encouraged medical personnel, public health advocates, scientists, and inventors to seek more effective and humane treatment. Advances in amputation techniques, infection control, and transport of patients all stem from Civil War medicine .... As a result, the late nineteenth and early twentieth centuries witnessed a wave of new medicines, tools, and technologies."

14. **B) is correct.** The author begins by relating events that happened in the 1840s and ends with "new medicines, tools, and technologies" of the "late nineteenth and early twentieth centuries."

15. **B) is correct.** The passage is mainly about "the beginnings of modern medicine," which began earlier than most people might think. The other sentences give details from the passage.

16. **D) is correct.** In the second paragraph, the author refers to "advances in amputation techniques" developed during the Civil War. Readers can infer that thousands of soldiers who had had limbs amputated as a result of war injuries needed prosthetics after the war was over.

17. **C) is correct.** In the third paragraph, the author writes, "The unprecedented bloodshed of the Civil War resulted in many medical innovations .... The sheer volume of medical need encouraged medical personnel, public health advocates, scientists, and inventors to seek more effective and humane treatment. Advances in amputation techniques, infection control, and transport of patients all stem from Civil War medicine. In addition, plastic surgery and prosthetics design took turns for the better after the war." Readers can infer that, even though the war killed many thousands of people, it was a positive event for modern medicine.

18. **A) is correct.** In the second paragraph, the author writes, "Before the discovery of anesthesia, patients had to merely endure as doctors sliced into their bodies with scalpels .... It was nearly impossible to carry out more advanced [surgery] while patients were writhing in pain." Readers can infer that by "merely endure," the author means that without anesthesia, patients had to just bear the pain "as doctors sliced into their bodies with scalpels."

19. **A) is correct.** The passage is mainly about the importance of the placenta. The other sentences give details from the passage.

20. **A) is correct.** In the second paragraph, the author writes, "[The placenta] exchanges nutrients between the blood supplies of the mother and the fetus—although the blood supplies do not intermingle throughout this process. Nutrients from the fetal blood and maternal blood are instead exchanged and regulated via blood vessels that filter each source without bringing them in direct contact." The context shows that the author uses the word *intermingle* to point out that the mother's blood and the fetus's blood do not come into direct contact—instead, the placenta acts as a "trading post."

21. **D) is correct.** The passage does not contain this detail. The author writes that "certain substances can pass through the placenta, causing problems for the developing fetus. Alcohol, tobacco, and drugs are among [these harmful] products."

22. **B) is correct.** The passage's primary purpose is informative. It is not persuasive or advisory. The author does mention the "trading post" metaphor, but this is a detail rather than a main idea or purpose for writing.

23. **C) is correct.** In the first sentence the author writes, "Aside from the uterus itself, the placenta is, perhaps, the most important organ directly involved with pregnancy."

24. **D) is correct.** In the second-to-last sentence, the author writes, "Certain substances can pass through the placenta, causing problems for the developing fetus." Readers can infer that if a mother smokes or consumes alcohol or drugs when she is pregnant, it can harm her baby. The seriousness of the harm probably depends on the amounts and kinds of substances the mother uses.

25. **A) is correct.** The passage is mainly about the link between the Zika virus and microcephaly. The other sentences give details from the passage.

26. **B) is correct.** In the first paragraph, the author writes, "A devastating condition ... microcephaly ... literally means 'small head.' It can occur when a fetus's brain stops developing in utero. There is no known cure, and many babies born with microcephaly have other problems as a result, such as developmental delays or loss of hearing or vision." Readers can use context to infer that by "a devastating condition," the author means "a condition that causes great harm" to a developing fetus.

27. **D) is correct.** The passage does not contain this detail. The author does not list countries or regions where the Zika virus may be found.

28. **B) is correct.** The passage is primarily informative, but there is an underlying cautionary message to take the microcephaly epidemic seriously. The passage is not reassuring, persuasive, or advisory.

29. **D) is correct.** In the last sentence of the first paragraph, the author writes that "scientists are working hard in their laboratories to better understand the connection between the Zika virus and microcephaly." Readers can infer that scientists need and/or want to know more about this connection, even though the link between Zika virus and microcephaly has already been established.

30. **D) is correct.** *Mosquito-borne* means "carried by mosquitoes." The author states that the "microcephaly epidemic is strongly correlated with the mosquito-borne disease known as the Zika virus." In the second paragraph the author writes that "evidence has shown that if a mother contracts Zika, either by being bitten by an infected mosquito or engaging in sexual activity with someone infected, the virus has the ability to cross the placental barrier between the mother and fetus." An "infected mosquito" carries Zika.

31. **B) is correct.** The passage is primarily informative. However, the author uses wordplay in the last sentence to entertain readers: "On one side, health organizations are saying take it easy on the hot dogs; on the other side, the meat industry is claiming it's all just baloney."

32. **C) is correct.** To entertain readers, the author is making a pun: "it's all just baloney" means "it's nonsense." But baloney is also a processed meat product that usually contains nitrates.

33.	**B) is correct.** As the title shows, the passage is mainly about the link between processed meats and cancer. The passage does not say that "most meats" cause cancer. The other two sentences provide details that support the main idea.

34.	**C) is correct.** In paragraph 2, the author writes, "Grilling and smoking these processed meats may produce even more cancer-causing compounds." Hotdogs are processed meats, and many brands contain nitrates.

35.	**D) is correct.** In the last sentence, the author writes, "On one side, health organizations are saying take it easy on the hot dogs." Readers can infer from context that the author means these organizations are counseling people not to eat an excessive number of hotdogs.

36.	**C) is correct.** In the second sentence, the author writes, "Americans ... are consuming twenty *more* teaspoons of sugar daily than the American Heart Association's recommendation of six teaspoons for women and nine for men."

37.	**A) is correct.** In the first sentence, the author writes, "Sugar is an essential fuel for the human body." Readers can infer from context that the author is using the word *fuel* to mean "energy source."

38.	**D) is correct.** This detail is not found in the passage. However, the author does mention that some processed foods contain added sugar.

39.	**A) is correct.** The text is primarily informative, although there is an underlying cautionary message about health problems that can result from consuming too much sugar.

40.	**B) is correct.** In the second sentence, the author writes that the American Heart Association recommends only six teaspoons of sugar per day for women, so twenty-six is probably far too much sugar per day unless the woman in question exercises constantly throughout the day.

41.	**C) is correct.** The author writes, "This new device is a pain-free vaccination tool that does not need refrigeration like some vaccines delivered via syringe. The tiny patch ... injects medications into the body's cells without injuring patients like hypodermic needles do." Readers can infer from this that using a patch is more convenient than using a hypodermic syringe needle for two reasons: 1) the patch does not need refrigeration, and 2) the patch is not painful, so it does not scare patients. The passage does not mention cost.

42.	**C) is correct.** The author seems excited about the new pain-free vaccination tool that biotechnology has produced. The passage is not primarily cautionary or advisory. The author does not tell a story about a specific doctor.

43.	**C) is correct.** The passage is mainly about the "new, transdermal vaccine delivery system." The other sentences give details from the passage.

44.	**D) is correct.** In the second paragraph, the author writes, "The creation of a new, transdermal vaccine delivery system may make the needle obsolete .... The tiny patch ... latches on to human skin via a spring-loading mechanism." Readers can infer that *trans* means "across or through," and *dermal* refers to human skin.

45.	**A) is correct.** In the second paragraph, the author writes, "Scientists believe transdermal vaccines may be able to supplant hypodermic needles for medical practitioners carrying out vaccination efforts in developing nations. While diseases like polio have been eradicated in the United States, they still affect populations in developing nations. This new technology could change the lives of millions of people around the globe."

46.   **B) is correct.** In the first and second paragraphs, the author writes, "Now biotechnologists are taking aim at one of the most fear-inducing medical instruments in history: the hypodermic syringe needle. The hypodermic syringe needle has been sticking patients since the 1850s, but the creation of a new, transdermal vaccine delivery system may make the needle obsolete." Readers can infer that the author thinks the "new, transdermal vaccine delivery system" will replace—or supplant—the hypodermic syringe needle, making the scary needle outdated and no longer necessary.

TWO: WRITING

Grammar

The English and Language Usage section will test your understanding of the basic rules of grammar. The first step in preparing for this section of the test is to review the parts of speech and the rules that accompany them. The good news is that you have been using these rules since you first began to speak. Even if you do not know a lot of the technical terms, many of these rules will be familiar to you. Some of the topics you might see include:

- matching pronouns with their antecedents
- matching verbs with their subjects
- ensuring that verbs are in the correct tense
- using correct capitalization
- distinguishing between types of sentences
- correcting sentence structure
- identifying parts of speech

NOUNS AND PRONOUNS

Nouns are people, places, or things. The subject of a sentence is typically a noun. For example, in the sentence "The hospital was very clean," the subject, *hospital*, is a noun; it is a place. **Pronouns** stand in for nouns and can be used to make sentences sound less repetitive. Take the sentence, "Sam stayed home from school because Sam was not feeling well." The word *Sam* appears twice in the same sentence. Instead, you can use the pronoun *he* to stand in for *Sam* and say, "Sam stayed home from school because he was not feeling well."

Because pronouns take the place of nouns, they need to agree both in number and gender with the noun they replace. So, a plural noun needs a plural pronoun, and a noun referring to something feminine needs a feminine pronoun. In the first sentence in this paragraph, for example, the plural pronoun *they* replaced the plural noun *pronouns*. There will usually be several questions on the English and Language Usage section that cover pronoun agreement, so it's good to get comfortable spotting pronouns.

Wrong: If a student forgets their homework, they will not receive a grade

Correct: If a student forgets his or her homework, he or she will not receive a grade.

Student is a singular noun, but *their* and *they* are plural pronouns. So, the first sentence is incorrect. To correct it, use the singular pronoun *his* or *her* or *he* or *she*.

Wrong: Everybody will receive their paychecks promptly.

Correct: Everybody will receive his or her paycheck promptly.

Everybody is a singular noun, but *their* is a plural pronoun. So, the first sentence is incorrect. To correct it, use the singular pronoun *his* or *her*.

Wrong: When nurses scrub in to surgery, you should wash your hands.

Correct: When nurses scrub in to surgery, they should wash their hands.

The first sentence begins in third-person perspective and then switches to second-person perspective. So, this sentence is incorrect. To correct it, use a third-person pronoun in the second clause.

Wrong: After the teacher spoke to the student, she realized her mistake.

Correct: After Mr. White spoke to his student, she realized her mistake. (*She* and *her* refer to the student.)

Correct: After speaking to the student, the teacher realized her own mistake. (*Her* refers to the teacher.)

The first sentence refers to a teacher and a student. But whom does *she* refer to, the teacher or the student? To eliminate the ambiguity, use specific names or state more specifically who made the mistake.

PRACTICE QUESTIONS

1. Which of the following lists includes all the nouns in the sentence?

    I have lived in Minnesota since August, but I still don't own a warm coat or gloves.

    A) coat, gloves

    B) I, coat, gloves

    C) Minnesota, August, coat, gloves

    D) I, Minnesota, August, warm, coat, gloves

2. In which of the following sentences do the nouns and pronouns not agree?

    A) After we walked inside, we took off our hats and shoes and hung them in the closet.

    B) The members of the band should leave her instruments in the rehearsal room.

    C) The janitor on duty should rinse out his or her mop before leaving for the day.

    D) When you see someone in trouble, you should always try to help them.

VERBS

A **verb** is the action of a sentence: it describes what the subject of the sentence is or is doing. Verbs must match the subject of the sentence in person and number, and must be in the proper tense—past, present, or future.

Person describes the relationship of the speaker to the subject of the sentence: first (I, we), second (you), and third (he, she, it, they). *Number* refers to whether the subject of the sentence is singular or plural. Verbs are conjugated to match the person and number of the subject.

HELPFUL HINT

Think of the subject and the verb as sharing a single s. If the subject ends with an s, the verb should not, and vice versa.

Table 2.1. Conjugating Verbs for Person

Person	Singular	Plural
First	I jump	we jump
Second	you jump	you jump
Third	he/she/it jumps	they jump

Wrong: The cat chase the ball while the dogs runs in the yard.

Correct: The cat chases the ball while the dogs run in the yard.

Cat is singular, so it takes a singular verb (which confusingly ends with an *s*); *dogs* is plural, so it needs a plural verb.

Wrong: The cars that had been recalled by the manufacturer was returned within a few months.

Correct: The cars that had been recalled by the manufacturer were returned within a few months.

Sometimes, the subject and verb are separated by clauses or phrases. Here, the subject *cars* is separated from the verb by the relatively long phrase "that had been recalled by the manufacturer," making it more difficult to determine how to correctly conjugate the verb.

Correct: The doctor and nurse work in the hospital.

Correct: Neither the nurse nor her boss was scheduled to take a vacation.

Correct: Either the patient or her parents need to sign the release forms.

When the subject contains two or more nouns connected by *and*, that subject becomes plural and requires a plural verb. Singular subjects joined by *or, either/or, neither/ nor,* or *not only/but also* remain singular; when these words join plural and singular subjects, the verb should match the closest subject.

Finally, verbs must be conjugated for tense, which shows when the action happened. Some conjugations include helping verbs like *was, have, have been,* and *will have been.*

HELPFUL HINT

If the subject is separated from the verb, cross out the phrases between them to make conjugation easier.

Table 2.2. Verb Tenses

Tense	Past	Present	Future
Simple	I <u>gave</u> her a gift yesterday.	I <u>give</u> her a gift every day.	I <u>will give</u> her a gift on her birthday.
Continuous	I <u>was giving</u> her a gift when you got here.	I <u>am giving</u> her a gift; come in!	I <u>will be giving</u> her a gift at dinner.
Perfect	I <u>had given</u> her a gift before you got there.	I <u>have given</u> her a gift already.	I <u>will have given</u> her a gift by midnight.
Perfect continuous	Her friends <u>had been giving</u> her gifts all night when I arrived.	I <u>have been giving</u> her gifts every year for nine years.	I <u>will have been giving</u> her gifts on holidays for ten years next year.

Tense must also be consistent throughout the sentence and the passage. For example, the sentence *I was baking cookies and eat some dough* sounds strange. That is because the two verbs, *was baking* and *eat*, are in different tenses. *Was baking* occurred in the past; *eat*, on the other hand, occurs in the present. To make them consistent, change *eat* to *ate*.

Wrong: Because it will rain during the party last night, we had to move the tables inside.

Correct: Because it rained during the party last night, we had to move the tables inside.

All the verb tenses in a sentence need to agree both with each other and with the other information in the sentence. In the first sentence above, the tense does not match the other information in the sentence: *last night* indicates the past (*rained*), not the future (*will rain*).

PRACTICE QUESTIONS

3. Which of the following sentences contains an incorrectly conjugated verb?
    A) The brother and sister runs very fast.
    B) Neither Anne nor Suzy likes the soup.
    C) The mother and father love their new baby.
    D) Either Jack or Jill will pick up the pizza.

4. Which of the following sentences contains an incorrect verb tense?
    A) After the show ended, we drove to the restaurant for dinner.
    B) Anne went to the mall before she headed home.
    C) Johnny went to the movies after he cleans the kitchen.
    D) Before the alarm sounded, smoke filled the cafeteria.

ADJECTIVES AND ADVERBS

Adjectives provide more information about a noun in a sentence. Take the sentence, "The boy hit the ball." If you want your readers to know more about the noun *boy*, you could use an adjective to describe him: *the little boy, the young boy, the tall boy.*

Adverbs and adjectives are similar because they provide more information about a part of a sentence. However, adverbs do not describe nouns—that's an adjective's job. Instead, adverbs describe verbs, adjectives, and even other adverbs. For example, in the sentence "The doctor had recently hired a new employee," the adverb *recently* tells us more about how the action *hired* took place.

Adjectives, adverbs, and **modifying phrases** (groups of words that together modify another word) should be placed as close as possible to the word they modify. Separating words from their modifiers can create incorrect or confusing sentences.

> **Wrong:** Running through the hall, the bell rang and the student knew she was late.
>
> **Correct:** Running through the hall, the student heard the bell ring and knew she was late.

The phrase *running through the hall* should be placed next to *student*, the noun it modifies.

The suffixes *–er* and *–est* are often used to modify adjectives when a sentence is making a comparison. The suffix *–er* is used when comparing two things, and the suffix *–est* is used when comparing more than two.

> Anne is taller than Steve, but Steve is more coordinated.
>
> Of the five brothers, Billy is the funniest, and Alex is the most intelligent.

Adjectives longer than two syllables are compared using *more* (for two things) or *most* (for three or more things).

> **Wrong:** Of my two friends, Clara is the smartest.
>
> **Correct:** Of my two friends, Clara is smarter.

More and *most* should not be used in conjunction with *–er* and *–est* endings.

> **Wrong:** My most warmest sweater is made of wool.
>
> **Correct:** My warmest sweater is made of wool.

PRACTICE QUESTIONS

5. Which of the following lists includes all the adjectives in the sentence?
    The new chef carefully stirred the boiling soup and then lowered the heat.
    A) new, boiling
    B) new, carefully, boiling
    C) new, carefully, boiling, heat
    D) new, carefully, boiling, lowered, heat

6. Which of the following sentences contains an adjective error?

A) The new red car was faster than the old blue car.

B) Reggie's apartment is in the tallest building on the block.

C) The slice of cake was tastier than the brownie.

D) Of the four speeches, Jerry's was the most long.

OTHER PARTS OF SPEECH

Prepositions express the location of a noun or pronoun in relation to other words and phrases described in a sentence. For example, in the sentence "The nurse parked her car in a parking garage," the preposition *in* describes the position of the car in relation to the garage. Together, the preposition and the noun that follow it are called a **prepositional phrase**. In this example, the prepositional phrase is "in a parking garage."

Conjunctions connect words, phrases, and clauses. The conjunctions summarized in the acronym FANBOYS—For, And, Nor, But, Or, Yet, So—are called **coordinating conjunctions** and are used to join **independent clauses** (clauses that can stand alone as a complete sentence). For example, in the following sentence, the conjunction *and* joins together two independent clauses:

> The nurse prepared the patient for surgery, <u>and</u> the doctor performed the surgery.

Other conjunctions, like *although*, *because*, and *if*, join together an independent and a **dependent clause** (which cannot stand on its own). Take the following sentence:

> She had to ride the subway <u>because her car was broken</u>.

The clause *because her car was broken* cannot stand on its own.

Interjections, like *wow* and *hey*, express emotion and are most commonly used in conversation and casual writing.

HELPFUL HINT

An independent (or main) clause can stand alone as its own sentence. A dependent (or subordinate) clause must be attached to an independent clause to make a complete sentence.

PRACTICE QUESTIONS

Choose the word that best completes the sentence.

7. Her love _____ blueberry muffins kept her coming back to the bakery every week.

A) to

B) with

C) of

D) about

8. Christine left her house early on Monday morning, _____ she was still late for work.

A) but

B) and

C) for

D) or

Sentence Structure

To understand what a phrase is, you have to know about subjects and predicates. The **subject** is what the sentence is about; the **predicate** contains the verb and its modifiers.

The nurse at the front desk will answer any questions you have.

Subject: the nurse at the front desk

Predicate: will answer any questions you have

A **phrase** is a group of words that communicates only part of an idea because it lacks either a subject or a predicate. Phrases are categorized based on the main word in the phrase. A **prepositional phrase** begins with a preposition and ends with an object of the preposition, a **verb phrase** is composed of the main verb along with any helping verbs, and a **noun phrase** consists of a noun and its modifiers.

Prepositional phrase: The dog is hiding under the porch.

Verb phrase: The chef wanted to cook a different dish.

Noun phrase: The big red barn rests beside the vacant chicken house.

PRACTICE QUESTION

9. Identify the type of phrase underlined in the following sentence.
   The new patient was assigned to the nurse with the most experience.
   A) prepositional phrase
   B) noun phrase
   C) verb phrase
   D) verbal phrase

CLAUSES

Clauses contain both a subject and a predicate. They can be either independent or dependent. An **independent** (or main) **clause** can stand alone as its own sentence.

The dog ate her homework.

Dependent (or subordinate) clauses cannot stand alone as their own sentences. They start with a subordinating conjunction, relative pronoun, or relative adjective, which will make them sound incomplete.

Because the dog ate her homework

A sentence can be classified as simple, compound, complex, or compound-complex based on the type and number of clauses it has.

Table 2.3. Sentences

Sentence type	Number of independent clauses	Number of dependent clauses
Simple	1	0
Compound	2 or more	0
Complex	1	1 or more
Compound-complex	2 or more	1 or more

A **simple sentence** consists of one independent clause. Because there are no dependent clauses in a simple sentence, it can be a two-word sentence, with one word being the subject and the other word being the verb, such as *I ran*. However, a simple sentence can also contain prepositions, adjectives, and adverbs. Even though these additions can extend the length of a simple sentence, it is still considered a simple sentence as long as it does not contain any dependent clauses.

HELPFUL HINT

On the test you will have to both identify and construct different kinds of sentences.

> San Francisco in the springtime is one of my favorite places to visit.

Although the sentence is lengthy, it is simple because it contains only one subject and one verb (*San Francisco* and *is*), modified by additional phrases.

Compound sentences have two or more independent clauses and no dependent clauses. Usually a comma and a coordinating conjunction (the FANBOYS: *For, And, Nor, But, Or, Yet*, and *So*) join the independent clauses, though semicolons can be used as well. The sentence "My computer broke, so I took it to be repaired" is compound.

> The game was canceled, but we will still practice on Saturday.

This sentence is made up of two independent clauses joined by a conjunction (*but*), so it is compound.

Complex sentences have one independent clause and at least one dependent clause. In the complex sentence "If you lie down with dogs, you'll wake up with fleas," the first clause is dependent (because of the subordinating conjunction *if*), and the second is independent.

QUICK REVIEW

Can you write a simple, compound, complex, and compound-complex sentence using the same independent clause?

> I love listening to the radio in the car because I can sing along as loud as I want.

> The sentence has one independent clause (*I love...car*) and one dependent (*because I...want*), so it is complex.

Compound-complex sentences have two or more independent clauses and at least one dependent clause. For example, the sentence *Even though David was a vegetarian, he went with his friends to steakhouses, but he focused on the conversation instead of the food*, is compound-complex.

I wanted to get a dog, but I have a fish because my roommate is allergic to pet dander.

This sentence has three clauses: two independent (*I wanted...dog* and *I have a fish*) and one dependent (*because my...dander*), so it is compound-complex.

PRACTICE QUESTIONS

10. Which of the following choices is a simple sentence?

A) Elsa drove while Erica navigated.

B) Betty ordered a fruit salad, and Sue ordered eggs.

C) Because she was late, Jenny ran down the hall.

D) John ate breakfast with his mother, brother, and father.

11. Which of the following sentences is a compound-complex sentence?

A) While they were at the game, Anne cheered for the home team, but Harvey rooted for the underdogs.

B) The rain flooded all of the driveway, some of the yard, and even part of the sidewalk across the street.

C) After everyone finished the test, Mr. Brown passed a bowl of candy around the classroom.

D) All the flowers in the front yard are in bloom, and the trees around the house are lush and green.

PUNCTUATION

The basic rules for using the major punctuation marks are given in the table below.

Table 2.4. How to Use Punctuation

Punctuation	Used for	Example
Period	ending sentences	Periods go at the end of complete sentences.
Question mark	ending questions	What's the best way to end a sentence?
Exclamation point	ending sentences that show extreme emotion	I'll never understand how to use commas!
Comma	joining two independent clauses (always with a coordinating conjunction)	Commas can be used to join clauses, but they must always be followed by a coordinating conjunction.
	setting apart introductory and nonessential words and phrases	Commas, when used properly, set apart extra information in a sentence.
	separating items in a list	My favorite punctuation marks include the colon, semicolon, and period.

Table 2.4. How to Use Punctuation (continued)

Punctuation	Used for	Example
Semicolon	joining together two independent clauses (never used with a conjunction)	I love exclamation points; they make sentences seem so exciting!
Colon	introducing a list, explanation, or definition	When I see a colon I know what to expect: more information.
Apostrophe	forming contractions	It's amazing how many people can't use apostrophes correctly.
	showing possession	Parentheses are my sister's favorite punctuation; she finds commas' rules confusing.
Quotation marks	indicating a direct quote	I said to her, "Tell me more about parentheses."

PRACTICE QUESTIONS

12. Which of the following sentences contains an error in punctuation?

    A) I love apple pie! John exclaimed with a smile.

    B) Jennifer loves Adam's new haircut.

    C) Billy went to the store; he bought bread, milk, and cheese.

    D) Alexandra hates raisins, but she loves chocolate chips.

13. Which punctuation mark correctly completes the sentence?

    *Sam, why don't you come with us for dinner_*

    A) .

    B) ?

    C) ;

    D) :

Homophones and Spelling

The exam may include questions that ask you to choose between **homophones**, words that are pronounced the same but have different meanings. *Bawl* and *ball*, for example, are homophones: they sound the same, but the first means "to cry," and the second is a round toy.

Common homophones include:

- bare/bear
- brake/break
- die/dye
- effect/affect
- flour/flower

- heal/heel
- insure/ensure
- morning/mourning
- peace/piece
- poor/pour
- principal/principle
- sole/soul
- stair/stare
- suite/sweet
- their/there/they're
- wear/where

You will also be tested on spelling, so it is good to familiarize yourself with commonly misspelled words and special spelling rules. The test questions will ask you to either find a misspelled word in a sentence or identify words that don't follow standard spelling rules.

Double a final consonant when adding suffixes if the consonant is preceded by a single vowel.

run → running
admit → admittance

Drop the final vowel when adding a suffix.

sue → suing
observe → observance

Change the final *y* to an *i* when adding a suffix.

lazy → laziest
tidy → tidily

Regular nouns are made plural by adding *s*. Irregular nouns can follow many different rules for pluralization, which are summarized in the table below.

TABLE 2.5. Irregular Plural Nouns

Ends with . . .	Make it plural by . . .	Example
y	changing *y* to *i* and adding –es	baby babies
f	changing *f* to *v* and adding –es	leaf leaves
fe	changing *f* to *v* and adding –s	knife knives
o	adding –es	potato potatoes

2.5. Irregular Plural Nouns (continued)

Ends with . . .	Make it plural by . . .	Example
us	changing –us to –i	nucleus nuclei

Always the same	Doesn't follow the rules
sheep	man men
deer	child children
fish	person people
moose	tooth teeth
pants	goose geese
binoculars	mouse mice
scissors	ox oxen

Commonly Misspelled Words

- accommodate
- across
- argument
- believe
- committee
- completely
- conscious
- discipline
- experience
- foreign
- government
- guarantee
- height
- immediately
- intelligence
- judgment
- knowledge
- license
- lightning
- lose
- maneuver
- misspell
- noticeable
- occasionally
- occurred
- opinion
- personnel
- piece
- possession
- receive
- separate
- successful
- technique
- tendency
- unanimous
- until
- usually
- vacuum
- whether
- which

Some words are similar in meaning but are not synonyms. However, they are commonly confused in writing and speech. A hallmark of good writing is the proper use of these words.

TABLE 2.6. Commonly Confused Words

Confused Words	Definition
Amount	describes a noncountable quantity (*an unknown amount of jewelry was stolen*)
Number	describes a countable quantity (*an unknown number of necklaces was stolen*)
Bring	toward the speaker (*bring to me*)
Take	away from the speaker (*take away from me*)
Farther	a measurable distance (*the house farther up the road*)
Further	more or greater (*explain further what you mean*)
Fewer	a smaller amount of something plural (*fewer chairs*)
Less	a smaller amount of something that cannot be counted (*less water*)
Lose	to fail to win; to not be able to find something (*to lose a game; to lose one's keys*)
Loose	relaxed; not firmly in place (*my pants are loose*)

PRACTICE QUESTIONS

14. Which of the following sentences contains a spelling error?

A) It was unusually warm that winter, so we didn't need to use our fireplace.

B) Our garden includes tomatos, squash, and carrots.

C) The local zoo will be opening a new exhibit that includes African elephants.

D) My sister is learning to speak a foreign language so she can travel abroad.

15. Which of the following words correctly completes the sentence?

The nurse has three _____ to see before lunch.

A) patents

B) patience

C) patients

D) patient's

16. Which of the following words correctly completes the sentence?

Without a proper chain of evidence, we could _____ the case.

A) lose

B) loose

C) loss

D) loses

17. Which of the following words correctly completes the sentence?

There were _____ cars this morning in the parking lot than usual.

A) less

B) fewer

C) several

D) enough

Writing Review Questions

1. Select the best words for the blanks in the following sentence.

Mateo was _____ busy studying for an exam _____ attend the party with his roommate.

A) too, too

B) two, too

C) to, two

D) too, to

2. Select the best words for the blank in the following sentence.

By the time Taylor arrived at the meeting, I was ready to leave. I _____ for her all evening.

A) had waited

B) have waited

C) had been waited

D) will wait

3. Select the best words for the blanks in the following sentence.

If _____ ready to leave now, please get _____ coat, and I'll pick you up at the front door.

A) your, our

B) you're, your

C) you're, hour

D) yore, you're

4. Select the best word for the blank in the second sentence.

Do you know the Raymer twins? _____ standing over there with their parents.

A) They

B) There

C) Their

D) They're

5. Select the best words for the blanks in the following sentence.

The _____ teammates were practicing _____ the big game on the following Friday.

A) fore, four

B) four, for

C) fewer, for

D) four, fore

6. Select the best word for the blank in the following sentence.

I can't go with you to the meeting tonight _____ I have too much work to complete for class.

A) yet

B) nor

C) because

D) although

7. Select the best word for the blank in the following sentence.

I'm convinced that there are _____ cookies on that plate than there were just an hour ago.

A) less

B) fewer

C) tastier

D) sweeter

8. Select the best word for the blank in the following sentence.

Who is a millennial? Researchers _____ that generation as those born between 1981 and 1996.

A) define

B) defend

C) defer

D) differ

9. Select the best word for the blank in the following sentence.

I sliced some _____ of bread for toast.

A) peas

B) peaces

C) pieces

D) appeases

10. Select the best word for the blank in the following sentence.

Queen Elizabeth II has _____ over the United Kingdom for over sixty-five years (since 1952, when her father died).

A) reined

B) rained

C) rayon

D) reigned

11. Select the best words for the blanks in the following sentence.

I _____ busy studying for my exam, and my brothers _____ busy studying for theirs.

A) are, are

B) are, am

C) am, am

D) am, are

12. Select the best word for the blank in the following sentence.

Last night, after dropping easy flyballs all evening, left-fielder Danny Pine finally _____ one in the last play of the game.

A) catched

B) caught

C) catches

D) catch

13. Select the best helping verbs for the blanks in the following sentence.

Because I _____ always wanted to stay at the Grand Hotel, my great-aunt _____ generously offered to take me and my sister there for a "girls' weekend."

A) have, has

B) was, is

C) have been, might

D) will have, have

14. Select the best word or phrase for the blank in the following sentence.

My dog _____ me happy every day.

A) make

B) makes

C) will have made

D) should have make

15. Select the best punctuation marks for the blanks in the following sentence.

"Jean ____" I asked, "Why don't you come over for dinner ____"

A) a colon and an exclamation point

B) a comma and a question mark

C) a semicolon and a period

D) a period and a question mark

16. Select the best punctuation mark for the blank in the following sentence.

"I wish we could go to Hawaii____" Adelaide said.

A) ?

B) .

C) ,

D) ;

17. Select the best punctuation marks for the blanks in the following sentence.

Older sister Hollie said she didn't like the way Katrina always answered ____No!" whenever Mom asked the little girl to do something____

A) an opening quotation mark and a period

B) a colon and a question mark

C) an opening quotation mark and an exclamation point

D) a semicolon and a period

18. Select the best punctuation mark for the blank in the following sentence.

I felt like asking, "What are we doing here, anyway____"

A) .

B) !

C) ?

D) ;

19. Select the best words for the blanks in the following sentence.

____ is nobody over ____. Did you think you saw someone?

A) They're their

B) Their, they're

C) They're, there

D) There, there

20. Select the best word for the blank in the following sentence.

Dad thought it was important to _____ our home in case of a fire.

A) ensure

B) insure

C) assure

D) assay

21. Select the best words for the blanks in the following sentence.

Our ____ says she lives by this ____: "Honesty is the best policy."

A) principle, principal

B) prince, principle

C) principal, invincible

D) principal, principle

22. Select the best word for the blank in the following sentence.

The boy was so tired that he fell asleep as soon as his mother _____ him down on the bed.

A) laid

B) lied

C) ley

D) lei

23. Select the best word for the blank in the following sentence.

I don't want to _____ my keys, so I put them in the same place every night.

A) loosen

B) loose

C) lose

D) lost

24. Select the best word for the blank in the following sentence.

Gold is a valuable precious _____ used in jewelry, medicine, and technology.

A) meddle

B) medal

C) mettle

D) metal

25. Select the best word for the blank in the following sentence.

At Andre's new job, he can only take _____ breaks during the workday.

A) to

B) too

C) two

D) tow

26. Select the best word for the blank in the following sentence.

Juanita could _____ gone out with her friends last night, but she stayed home to study.

A) of

B) have

C) had

D) ave

27. Select the best word for the blank in the following sentence.

Mr. Henderson, a kind, fair _____, coached us in physical education at recess time.

A) Man

B) men

C) man

D) main

28. Select the best words for the blanks in the following sentence.

One medication _____ me poorly, but the other medication had no _____ at all.

A) effected; affect

B) affected; effect

C) effected; effect

D) affected; affect

29. Select the best words for the blank in the following sentence.

When I was in second grade, my _____ moved away to New Mexico.

A) best friend Jill

B) Best Friend Jill

C) best Friend Jill

D) best friend jill

30. Select the best word for the blank in the following sentence.

The tests determined there were _____ drugs in the patient's blood.

A) unjust

B) injust

C) elicit

D) illicit

31. Select the best word for the blank in the following sentence.

In _____ we always go camping in Yosemite National Park.

A) sooner

B) summer

C) sunner

D) sunnier

32. Select the best word for the blank in the following sentence.

The experienced nurse was _____ by the grisly wound on the patient's leg.

A) unphased

B) unfazed

C) unplaced

D) unfaced

33. Select the best word or phrase for the blank in the following sentence.

By the time Emma arrived at my house, we _____ already late for the party, so I was irritated with her.

A) were

B) was

C) had been

D) were being

34. Select the best words for the blanks in the following sentence.

After I _____ taking ice-skating lessons for two years, my coach _____ I was ready to move up into the next level, the Advanced Beginners.

A) might have been; had said

B) should have been; will say

C) will have been; says

D) had been; said

35. Select the best word for the blank in the following sentence.

In the future, whenever I think about my mom, I _____ that she is my hero.

A) realize

B) will realize

C) will have realized

D) had realized

1. **C) is correct.** *Minnesota* and *August* are proper nouns, and *coat* and *gloves* are common nouns. *I* is a pronoun, and *warm* is an adjective that modifies *coat*.

2. **B) is correct.** "The members of the band" is plural, so it should be replaced by the plural pronoun *their* instead of the singular *her*.

3. **A) is correct.** Choice A should read "The brother and sister run very fast." When the subject contains two or more nouns connected by *and*, the subject is plural and requires a plural verb.

4. **C) is correct.** Choice C should read "Johnny will go to the movies after he cleans the kitchen." It does not make sense to say that Johnny does something in the past (*went to the movies*) after doing something in the present (*after he cleans*).

5. **A) is correct.** *New* modifies the noun *chef*, and *boiling* modifies the noun *soup*. *Carefully* is an adverb modifying the verb *stirred*. *Lowered* is a verb, and *heat* is a noun.

6. **D) is correct.** Choice D should read, "Of the four speeches, Jerry's was the longest." The word *long* has only one syllable, so it should be modified with the suffix *–est*, not the word *most*.

7. **C) is correct.** The correct preposition is *of*.

8. **A) is correct.** In this sentence, the conjunction is joining together two contrasting ideas, so the correct answer is *but*.

9. **A) is correct.** The underlined section of the sentence is a prepositional phrase beginning with the preposition *with*.

10. **D) is correct.** Choice D contains one independent clause with one subject and one verb. Choices A and C are complex sentences because they each contain both a dependent and independent clause. Choice B contains two independent clauses joined by a conjunction and is therefore a compound sentence.

11. **A) is correct.** Choice A is a compound-complex sentence because it contains two independent clauses and one dependent clause. Despite its length, choice B is a simple sentence because it contains only one independent clause. Choice C is a complex sentence because it contains one dependent clause and one independent clause. Choice D is a compound sentence; it contains two independent clauses.

12. **A) is correct.** Choice A should use quotation marks to set off a direct quote: *"I love apple pie!" John exclaimed with a smile.*

13. **B) is correct.** The sentence is a question, so it should end with a question mark.

14. **B) is correct.** *Tomatos* should be spelled *tomatoes*.

15. **C) is correct.** *Patients* is the correct spelling and the correct homophone. A *patent* is proof that someone owns the rights to an invention or idea. *Patience* is the ability to avoid getting upset in negative situations. *Patient's*, which contains an apostrophe, is the singular possessive form of *patient*.

16.   **A) is correct.** To *lose* is to fail to *win*. *Loose* means "not firmly in place." *Loss* is a noun, and *loses* is incorrectly conjugated; neither choice makes sense in context.

17.   **B) is correct.** *Fewer* is used to indicate a smaller amount of something plural (in this case, cars). *Less* is used to indicate a smaller amount of something that cannot be counted (for instance, water or air). *Several* and *enough* do not make sense in context.

1. **D) is correct.** The correct answers are *too* and *to*. The adverb *too* correctly modifies the adjective *busy*. *To* combined with *attend* forms the infinitive verb *to attend*.

2. **A) is correct.** The sentence uses the past-perfect verb *had waited* to show that one past event ("I had waited for her all evening") happened before a second past event ("Taylor arrived").

3. **B) is correct.** The correct answers are *you're* and *your*. The contraction *you're* ("you are") correctly completes the phrase "if you're ready." The possessive pronoun *your* correctly completes the phrase "please get your coat."

4. **D) is correct.** The second sentence begins with the contraction *They're*, which means "They are." This contraction correctly completes the phrase "They're standing over there." Each of the other choices forms a grammatically incorrect sentence.

5. **B) is correct..** The adjective *four* correctly modifies *teammates*. The preposition *for* correctly completes the phrase "practicing for the big game."

6. **C) is correct.** The conjunction because correctly connects the opening independent clause "I can't go with you to the meeting tonight" to the dependent clause "because I have too much work to complete for class." It provides a cause-and-effect relationship between the two clauses. Choices A and B, *yet* and *nor*, must both be preceded by a comma. They also describe a contrasting relationship rather than a cause-and-effect relationship. Choice D, *although*, is nonsensical here because it too implies a contrasting relationship between the clauses rather than a cause-and-effect relationship.

7. **B) is correct.** The comparative adjective *fewer* describes a smaller number of items. *Less* describes a smaller amount of something that cannot be counted (such as water or milk). Neither *tastier* nor *sweeter* makes as much sense in the sentence, although each could be grammatically correct. It is more likely that there are fewer cookies than that the cookies became sweeter or tastier.

8. **A) is correct.** The verb *define* explains how researchers would characterize a generation. Choice B, *defend*, meaning "to protect or drive danger away from," does not make sense here; there is no danger. Choice C, *defer*, meaning "to postpone or delay," also does not make sense. Choice D, *differ*, means "to be unlike" someone or something and is nonsensical in the context of the sentence.

9. **C) is correct.** The sentence correctly uses the plural noun *pieces* to complete the phrase "pieces of bread." In choice A, *peas* are "a small green legume." In choice B, *peace* means "quiet and tranquility." In choice D, the verb *appeases* means "soothes, mollifies, or placates." None of these other words make sense in the sentence.

10. **D) is correct.** The sentence correctly uses the past-tense verb *reigned* (meaning "ruled"). In choice A, the verb *reined* means "to control or guide an animal such as a horse with leather reins." In choice B, the verb *rained* means "falling down in mass quantities." In choice C, *rayon* is a type of synthetic cloth. None of these other choices make sense in the sentence.

11. **D) is correct.** The correct answers are *am* and *are* in choice D. The singular first-person subject pronoun *I* matches *am*, the singular first-person form of the verb *to be*. The plural third-person subject *my brothers* matches *are*, the plural third-person form of the verb *to be*.

12. **B) is correct.** The verb *to catch* is irregular, and its past-tense form is *caught*. Choice A is incorrect: there is no such word as *catched*. Choice C incorrectly uses a present-tense verb, *catches*, in a sentence in which the action takes place "last night." Choice D incorrectly matches a singular noun, *Danny Pine*, with a plural verb, *catch*. Also, *catch* is a present-tense verb, and this sentence's action takes place "last night."

13. **A) is correct.** The correct answers are *have* and *has*. The other helping-verb choices all create incorrect, ungrammatical phrases such as "I was always wanted to stay" and "my great-aunt is generously offered to take me."

14. **B) is correct.** The singular present-tense verb *makes* makes sense in the sentence "My dog makes me happy every day." Choice A incorrectly matches a singular subject, *dog*, with a plural verb, *make*. Choice C does not make sense: the future-perfect verb "will have made" clashes with the phrase "every day" (which suggests the present). Choice D is incorrectly written. The conditional past-tense verb should be written "should have *made*," not "should have *make*."

15. **B) is correct.** The correct answers are a comma and a question mark. Correctly completed, the sentence looks like this: *"Jean," I asked, "Why don't you come over for dinner?"* Choice A is incorrect because a quotation cannot end in a colon. A colon denotes that the two sentence parts are closely related. In addition, the second half of the quotation is a question, which means an exclamation point is not the correct choice. Choice C is incorrect because a quotation cannot end in a semicolon and because a semicolon can only be used to join two complete independent clauses or items in a list. A question should not end in a period. Choice D is incorrect because a comma is used when attaching a speaker tag (*I asked*) to a quotation.

16. **C) is correct.** Choice C is correct because the quotation is a statement with a speaker tag attached. Commas are used to attach a speaker tag to a quotation that is a declarative statement. In choice A, the question mark is incorrect because the speaker is not asking a question. Choice B is incorrect because a period incorrectly separates the quotation from the speaker tag (*Adelaide said*). Choice D is incorrect because a semicolon is only used to join two complete independent clauses or items in a list.

17. **A) is correct.** The correct answers are an opening quotation mark and a period. Correctly completed, the sentence looks like this: *Older sister Hollie said she didn't like the way Katrina always answered "No!" whenever Mom asked the little girl to do something.* The quotation must have an opening quotation mark to indicate that Katrina is speaking. The sentence ends with a period because it is declarative. Choice B does not provide the opening quotation mark that is needed to match the closing quotation mark, and a question mark is incorrect because the sentence is a statement, not a question. Choice C might be possible, but the sentence does not deliver a specifically emotional or startling exclamation, so a period is more appropriate than an exclamation point. Choice D does not provide opening quotation marks to match the closing quotation marks, and a semicolon would incorrectly separate the speaker and the quotation.

18. **C) is correct.** The correct choice is C (a question mark). Correctly completed, the sentence looks like this: *I felt like asking, "What are we doing here, anyway?"* The sentence indicates a question with the word *asking* in the speaker tag, which means that only a question mark can correctly complete the sentence. None of the other punctuation marks are appropriate to use with an interrogative sentence.

19. **D) is correct.** The correct answers are *There* and *there*. The word *there* is an indefinite pronoun that indicates a place, as called for in the sentence context. The contraction *they're* means "they are," and *their* is a plural possessive pronoun. Correctly completed, the sentences look like this: *There is nobody over there. Did you think you saw someone?* Each of the other choices would result in an ungrammatical sentence.

20. **B) is correct.** The verb *insure* means "to cover with an insurance policy." None of the other choices make sense in the sentence. Choice A, *ensure*, means "to guarantee." Choice C, *assure*, means "to dispel any doubts." Choice D, *assay*, means "to determine content or quality."

21. **D) is correct.** The correct answers are *principal* and *principle*. A *principal* is the head of a school, and a *principle* is a value or maxim. In choice B, the masculine noun *prince* does not agree with the feminine pronoun *she*. In choice C, the adjective *invincible* (meaning "unbeatable") does not make sense in the sentence.

22. **A) is correct.** The verb *laid* is the past tense of *lay*, which means "to set or put down." Choice B, *lied*, is the past tense of the verb *lie*, meaning "to assert something that is untrue." *Ley* is a noun that refers to pasture, and a *lei* is a wreath made of flowers. None of these answer choices make sense in the context of the sentence.

23. **C) is correct.** The verb *lose* means "to be deprived of [something]" or "to have something go missing." To *loosen* is "to make something less tight," and *loose* is an antonym of *tight*. The verb *lost* is the past tense of *to lose* and does not make sense grammatically in this context because the sentence is written in the present tense.

24. **D) is correct.** A *metal* is an element like gold or silver. *Metal* also refers colloquially to many hard substances. The verb *meddle* means "to interfere with [something]." A *medal* is an award. Gold might be used to make a medal, but it is not a medal by itself. The noun *mettle* refers to a person's grit or determination. None of these answer choices make sense in the context of the sentence.

25. **C) is correct.** Choice C, the adjective *two* is correct. This choice refers to the number; Andre can take more than one break but less than three. The blank requires an adjective, and the number makes sense in context. *To* is a preposition that indicates direction, position, or purpose. *Too* is an adverb meaning "in addition" or "also." The verb *tow* means "to drag or pull behind"; a car might tow a trailer, for instance. None of the other three choices make sense in the context of the sentence.

26. **B) is correct.** *Could* is a helping verb, and it must be followed by the verb *have* for the entire phrase to make sense. Using choice A, *of*, is a common mistake in English grammar. However, it is incorrect; *of* is a preposition that indicates relationships, origin, and other functions. In choice C, the verb *had* does not match the helping verb *could*. Choice D, *ave*, is incorrect; to form the contraction, both the *h* and the *a* should be removed from *have* and an apostrophe added: *could've*.

27.   **C) is correct.** Here, the word *man* is a common noun, so it should be lowercased (which is why choice A is incorrect). Choice B incorrectly matches the singular proper noun *Mr. Henderson* with a plural noun, *men.* Choice D, *main* (an adjective meaning "chief in size or importance") does not make sense in the sentence.

28.   **B) is correct.** The verb *affect* means "to have an impact on [someone or something]." The noun *effect* means "result" or "impact." Choice A is incorrect. These words are commonly confused. *Effect* can be used as a verb, meaning "to make something happen" (for instance, "to effect change"). Likewise, *affect* can be used as a noun, most commonly in psychological contexts describing someone's demeanor: "the patient had a flat affect." These uses are far less common. It makes more sense for a medication to have an impact on a person, and a medication cannot have a demeanor, so choice B is a better choice than A. Choice C incorrectly uses the verb *effected,* and choice D incorrectly uses the noun *affect.*

29.   **A) is correct.** Here, *best* is a common adjective, *friend* is a common noun, and *Jill* is a proper noun. The other choices are incorrectly capitalized and/or lowercased.

30.   **D) is correct.** The adjective *illicit* means "unlawful"—the test revealed that the patient had taken, or somehow been exposed to, illegal drugs. *Unjust* means "unfair," and *injust* is a misspelling of *unjust*—it is not a word. *Elicit* is a verb that means "to draw from" or "to bring out." It is commonly confused with *illicit.*

31.   **B) is correct.** The names of seasons are common nouns, so *summer* is correctly lowercased. Choice A, the adverb *sooner,* does not make sense in this context. Choice C, *sunner,* is not a word—it might be a misspelling of the adjective in choice D, *sunnier,* which also does not make sense in the sentence.

32.   **B) is correct.** Choice B, the verb *unfazed* (meaning "undisturbed" or "undaunted"), is correct. An experienced nurse is unlikely to be put off by a gruesome wound; he or she would set aside any personal discomfort and focus on helping the patient. *Unphased* (meaning "not organized or structured in any chronological order") is a homonym of *unfazed;* the words are frequently confused. *Unplaced* means "not placed" and would not make sense in this context. *Unfaced* means "not having a facing," usually in reference to a wall or other surface, and it would not make sense in the context of this sentence.

33.   **A) is correct.** The plural verb *were* agrees with the plural subject pronoun *we.* Choices B, C, and D are all ungrammatical. Choice B is a singular verb. Choice C is past-perfect progressive, which indicates that the action was ongoing in the past, but before the other action—it is awkward and goes too far into the past. Choice D is past progressive, which also indicates an ongoing action in the past.

34.   **D) is correct.** The correct answer is choice D: *had been* and *said.* The correctly completed sentence uses the continuous past-perfect verb *had been taking* to show that one past event ("my coach said") happened after a second past event ("I had been taking ice-skating lessons"). The other answer choices use incorrect tenses to show the order of events.

35.   **B) is correct.** The future-tense verb *will realize* shows that one future event ("whenever I think about my mom") will have happened before a second future event ("I will realize . . . hero"). None of the other choices use the correct future tense.

THREE: MATHEMATICS

Types of Numbers

Numbers are placed in categories based on their properties.

- A **natural number** is greater than zero and has no decimal or fraction attached. These are also sometimes called counting numbers. {1, 2, 3, 4, ...}

- **Whole numbers** are natural numbers and the number zero. {0, 1, 2, 3, 4, ...}

- **Integers** include positive and negative natural numbers and zero. {. . ., −4, −3, −2, −1, 0, 1, 2, 3, 4, ...}

- A **rational number** can be represented as a fraction. Any decimal part must terminate or resolve into a repeating pattern. Examples include −12, −$\frac{4}{5}$, 0.36, 7.$\overline{7}$, 26$\frac{1}{2}$, etc.

- An **irrational number** cannot be represented as a fraction. An irrational decimal number never ends and never resolves into a repeating pattern. Examples include −$\sqrt{7}$, π, and 0.34567989135 ...

- A **real number** is a number that can be represented by a point on a number line. Real numbers include all the rational and irrational numbers.

HELPFUL HINT

If a real number is a natural number (e.g. 50), then it is also an integer, a whole number, and a rational number.

Every natural number (except 1) is either a prime number or a composite number. A **prime number** is a natural number greater than 1 which can only be divided evenly by 1 and itself. For example, 7 is a prime number because it can only be divided by the numbers 1 and 7.

On the other hand, a **composite number** is a natural number greater than 1 which can be evenly divided by at least one other number besides 1 and itself. For example, 6 is a composite number because it can be divided by 1, 2, 3, and 6.

Composite numbers can be broken down into prime numbers using factor trees. For example, the number 54 is 2 × 27, and 27 is 3 × 9, and 9 is 3 × 3, as shown in Figure 3.1.

Once the number has been broken down into its simplest form, the composite number can be expressed as a product of prime factors. Repeated factors can be written using exponents. An **exponent** shows how many times a number should be multiplied by itself. As shown in the factor tree, the number 54 can be written as 2 × 3 × 3 × 3 or 2 × 3³.

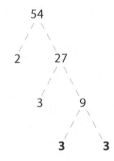

**Figure 3.1.
Factor Tree**

Scientific Notation

Scientific notation is a method of representing very large and small numbers in the form $a \times 10^n$ where a is a value between 1 and 10, and n is an integer. For example, the number 927,000,000 is written in scientific notation as 9.27×10^8. Multiplying 9.27 by 10 eight times gives 927,000,000. When performing operations with scientific notation, the final answer should be in the form $a \times 10^n$.

Table 3.1. Place Value

1,000,000	100,000	10,000	1,000	100	10	1	•	$\frac{1}{10}$	$\frac{1}{100}$
10^6	10^5	10^4	10^3	10^2	10^1	10^0		10^{-1}	10^{-2}
Millions	Hundred Thousands	Ten Thousands	Thousands	Hundreds	Tens	Ones	Decimal	Tenths	Hundreths

When adding and subtracting numbers in scientific notation, the power of 10 must be the same for all numbers. This results in like terms in which the a terms are added or subtracted and the 10^n remains unchanged. When multiplying numbers in scientific notation, multiply the a factors and add the exponents. For division, divide the a factors and subtract the exponents.

Positive and Negative Numbers

Positive numbers are greater than zero, and **negative numbers** are less than zero. Both positive and negative numbers can be shown on a **number line**.

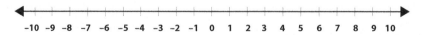

-10 -9 -8 -7 -6 -5 -4 -3 -2 -1 0 1 2 3 4 5 6 7 8 9 10

Figure 3.2. Number Line

Positive and negative numbers can be added, subtracted, multiplied, and divided. The sign of the resulting number is governed by a specific set of rules shown in the table below.

Table 3.2. Operations with Positive and Negative Numbers

Adding Real Numbers

Positve + Positive = Positive	$7 + 8 = 15$
Negative + Negative = Negative	$-7 + (-8) = -15$
Negative + Positive = Keep the sign of the number with the larger absolute value	$-7 + 8 = 1$ $7 + (-8) = -1$

Subtracting Real Numbers

Change the subtraction to addition, change the sign of the second number, and use addition rules.	
Negative − Positive = Negative	$-7 - 8 = -7 + (-8) = -15$
Positive − Negative = Positive	$7 - (-8) = 7 + 8 = 15$
Negative − Negative = Keep the sign of the number with the larger absolute value.	$-7 - (-8) = -7 + 8 = 1$ $-8 - (-7) = -8 + 7 = -1$
Positive − Positive = Positive if the first number is larger Negative if the second number is larger	$8 - 4 = 4$ $4 - 8 = -4$

Multiplying Real Numbers

Positive × Positive = Positive	$8 \times 4 = 32$
Negative × Negative = Positive	$-8 \times (-4) = 32$
Negative × Positive = Negative	$8 \times (-4) = -32$ $-8 \times 4 = -32$

Dividing Real Numbers

Positive ÷ Positive = Positive	$8 \div 4 = 2$
Negative ÷ Negative = Positive	$-8 \div (-4) = 2$
Positive ÷ Negative OR Negative ÷ Positive = Negative	$8 \div (-4) = -2$ $-8 \div 4 = -2$

PRACTICE QUESTIONS

Add or subtract the following real numbers:

6. $-18 + 12$

7. $-3.64 + (-2.18)$

8. $9.37 - 4.25$

9. $86 - (-20)$

Multiply or divide the following real numbers:

10. $\frac{10}{3}\left(-\frac{9}{5}\right)$

11. $\frac{-64}{-10}$

12. $(2.2)(3.3)$

13. $-52 \div 13$

Order of Operations

When solving a multi-step equation, the **order of operations** must be used to get the correct answer. Generally speaking, the problem should be worked in the following order: 1) parentheses and brackets; 2) exponents and square roots; 3) multiplication and division; 4) addition and subtraction. The acronym PEMDAS can be used to remember the order of operations.

Please Excuse (**My Dear**) (**Aunt Sally**)

1. **P** — Parentheses: Calculate expressions inside parentheses, brackets, braces, etc.

2. **E** — Exponents: Calculate exponents and square roots.

3. **M** — Multiply and **D** — Divide: Calculate any remaining multiplication and division in order from left to right.

4. **A** — Add and **S** — Subtract: Calculate any remaining addition and subtraction in order from left to right.

The steps "Multiply-Divide" and "Addition-Subtraction" go in order from left to right. In other words, divide before multiplying if the division problem is on the left.

For example, the expression $(3^2 - 2)^2 + (4)5^3$ is simplified using the following steps:

1. Parentheses: Because the parentheses in this problem contain two operations (exponents and subtraction), use the order of operations within the parentheses. Exponents come before subtraction. $(3^2 - 2)^2 + (4)5^3 = (9 - 2)^2 + (4)5^3 = (7)^2 + (4)5^3$

2. Exponents: $(7)^2 + (4)5^3 = 49 + (4)125$

3. Multiplication and division: $49 + (4)125 = 49 + 500$

4. Addition and subtraction: $49 + 500 = 549$

PRACTICE QUESTIONS

14. Simplify: $2(21 - 14) + 6 \div (-2) \times 3 - 10$

15. Simplify: $-3^2 + 4(5) + (5 - 6)^2 - 8$

16. Simplify: $\dfrac{(7 - 9)^3 + 8(10 - 12)}{4^2 - 5^2}$

Decimals and Fractions

DECIMALS

A **decimal** is a number that contains a decimal point. The place value for a decimal includes **tenths** (one place after the decimal point), **hundredths** (two places after the decimal point), **thousandths** (three places after the decimal point), etc.

5	4	•	3	2
5×10^1	4×10^0		3×10^{-1}	2×10^{-2}
5×10	4×1		$3 \times \frac{1}{10}$	$2 \times \frac{1}{100}$
50	4		0.3	0.02
Tens	Ones	Decimal Point	Tenths	Hundredths

$$50 + 4 + 0.3 + 0.02 = 54.32$$

Figure 3.3. Decimals and Place Value

Decimals can be added, subtracted, multiplied, and divided:

To add or subtract decimals, line up the decimal points and perform the operation, keeping the decimal point in the same place in the answer.

$$
\begin{array}{r}
12.35 \\
+\ 3.63 \\
\hline
=\ 15.98
\end{array}
$$

To multiply decimals, first multiply the numbers without the decimal points. Then, add the number of decimal places to the right of the decimal point in the original numbers and place the decimal point in the answer so that there are that many places to the right of the decimal.

$$12.35 \times 3.63 =$$
$$1235 \times 363 = 448305 \rightarrow 44.8305$$

HELPFUL HINT

If you're unsure which way to move the decimal after multiplying, remember that changing the decimal should always make the final answer smaller.

When dividing decimals, move the decimal point to the right in order to make the divisor a whole number and move the decimal the same number of places in the dividend. Divide the numbers without regard to the decimal. Then, place the decimal point of the quotient directly above the decimal point of the dividend.

$$\frac{12.35}{3.63} = \frac{1235}{363} =$$

$$
\begin{array}{r}
3.4 \\
363\,\overline{)1235.0}
\end{array}
$$

PRACTICE QUESTIONS

17. Simplify: 24.38 + 16.51 − 29.87

18. Simplify: $(10.4)(18.2)$

19. Simplify: $80 \div 2.5$

FRACTIONS

A **fraction** is a number that can be written in the form $\frac{a}{b}$ where b is not equal to zero. The a part of the fraction is the numerator (top number) and b part of the fraction is the denominator (bottom number).

If the denominator of a fraction is greater than the numerator, the value of the fraction is less than 1 and it is called a **proper fraction** (e.g., $\frac{3}{5}$ is a proper fraction).

In an **improper fraction**, the denominator is less than the numerator and the value of the fraction is greater than one (e.g., $\frac{8}{3}$ is an improper fraction). An improper fraction can be written as a whole number or a mixed number. A **mixed number** has a whole number part and a proper fraction part. Improper fractions can be converted to mixed numbers by dividing the numerator by the denominator, which gives the whole number part, and the remainder becomes the numerator of the proper fraction part (for example: improper fraction $\frac{25}{9}$ is equal to mixed number $2\frac{7}{9}$ because 9 divides into 25 two times, with a remainder of 7).

Conversely, mixed numbers can be converted to improper fractions. To do so, determine the numerator of the improper fraction by multiplying the denominator by the whole number, then adding the numerator. The final number is written as the (now larger) numerator over the original denominator.

Fractions with the same denominator can be added or subtracted by simply adding or subtracting the numerators; the denominator will remain unchanged. If the fractions to be added or subtracted do not have a common denominator, the least common multiple of the denominators must be found. The quickest way to find a common denominator of a set of values is simply to multiply all the values together. The result might not be the least common denominator, but it will get the job done.

In the operation $\frac{2}{3} - \frac{1}{2}$, the common denominator will be a multiple of both 3 and 2. Multiples are found by multiplying the denominator by whole numbers until a common multiple is found:

- multiples of 3 are **3** (3×1), **<u>6</u>** (3×2), **9** (3×3) ...
- multiples of 2 are **2** (2×1), **4** (2×2), **<u>6</u>** (2×3) ...

Since 6 is the smallest multiple of both 3 and 2, it is the least common multiple and can be used as the common denominator. Both the numerator and denominator of each fraction should be multiplied by the appropriate whole number:

$$\frac{2}{3}\left(\frac{2}{2}\right) - \frac{1}{2}\left(\frac{3}{3}\right) = \frac{4}{6} - \frac{3}{6} = \frac{1}{6}.$$

When multiplying fractions, simply multiply each numerator together and each denominator together, reducing the result if possible. To divide two fractions, invert the second fraction (swap the numerator and denominator), then multiply normally. If there are any mixed numbers when multiplying or dividing, they should first be changed to improper fractions. Note that multiplying proper fractions creates a value smaller than either original value.

HELPFUL HINT

$a\frac{m}{n} = \frac{n \times a + m}{n}$

$$\frac{5}{6} \times \frac{2}{3} = \frac{10}{18} = \frac{5}{9}$$

$$\frac{5}{6} \div \frac{2}{3} = \frac{5}{6} \times \frac{3}{2} = \frac{15}{12} = \frac{5}{4}$$

PRACTICE QUESTIONS

20. Simplify: $2\frac{3}{5} + 3\frac{1}{4} - 1\frac{1}{2}$

21. Simplify: $\frac{7}{8}(3\frac{1}{3})$

22. Simplify: $4\frac{1}{2} \div \frac{2}{3}$

CONVERTING BETWEEN FRACTIONS AND DECIMALS

A fraction is converted to a decimal by using long division until there is no remainder or a pattern of repeating numbers occurs.

$$\frac{1}{2} = 1 \div 2 = 0.5$$

To convert a decimal to a fraction, place the numbers to the right of the decimal over the appropriate base-10 power and simplify the fraction.

$$0.375 = \frac{375}{1000} = \frac{3}{8}$$

PRACTICE QUESTIONS

23. Write the fraction $\frac{7}{8}$ as a decimal.

24. Write the fraction $\frac{5}{11}$ as a decimal.

25. Write the decimal 0.125 as a fraction.

Rounding and Estimation

Rounding is a way of simplifying a complicated number. The result of rounding will be a less precise value that is easier to write or perform operations on. Rounding is performed to a specific place value, such as the thousands or tenths place.

The rules for rounding are as follows:

1. Underline the place value being rounded to.

2. Locate the digit one place value to the right of the underlined value. If this value is less than 5, keep the underlined value and replace all digits to the right of the underlined value with zero. If the value to the right of the underlined digit is more than 5, increase the underlined digit by one and replace all digits to the right of it with zero.

Estimation is when numbers are rounded and then an operation is performed. This process can be used when working with large numbers to find a close, but not exact, answer.

HELPFUL HINT

Estimation can often be used to eliminate answer choices on multiple choice tests without having to completely work the problem.

Ratios

A **ratio** is a comparison of two numbers and can be represented as $\frac{a}{b}$ ($b \neq 0$), $a{:}b$, or a to b. The two numbers represent a constant relationship, not a specific value: for every a number of items in the first group, there will be b number of items in the second. For example, if the ratio of blue to red candies in a bag is 3:5, the bag will contain 3 blue candies for every 5 red candies. So the bag might contain 3 blue candies and 5 red candies, or it might contain 30 blue candies and 50 red candies, or 36 blue candies and 60 red candies. All of these values are representative of the ratio 3:5 (which is the ratio in its lowest, or simplest, terms).

To find the "whole" when working with ratios, simply add the values in the ratio. For example, if the ratio of boys to girls in a class is 2:3, the "whole" is five: 2 out of every 5 students are boys, and 3 out of every 5 students are girls.

Proportions

A **proportion** is an equation which states that two ratios are equal. Proportions are given in the form $\frac{a}{b} = \frac{c}{d}$, where the a and d terms are the extremes and the b and c terms are the means. A proportion is solved using **cross-multiplication** to create an equation with no fractional components: $\frac{a}{b} = \frac{c}{d} \rightarrow ad = bc$

Percentages

A **percent** (or percentage) means per hundred and is expressed with a percent symbol (%). For example, 54% means 54 out of every 100. A percent can be converted to a decimal by removing the % symbol and moving the decimal point two places to the left, while a decimal can be converted to a percent by moving the decimal point two places to the right and attaching the % sign.

A percent can be converted to a fraction by writing the percent as a fraction with 100 as the denominator and reducing. A fraction can be converted to a percent by performing the indicated division, multiplying the result by 100 and attaching the % sign.

The percent equation has three variables: the part, the whole, and the percent (which is expressed in the equation as a decimal). The equation, as shown below, can be rearranged to solve for any of these variables.

$$\text{part} = \text{whole} \times \text{percent}$$

$$\text{percent} = \frac{\text{part}}{\text{whole}}$$

$$\text{whole} = \frac{\text{part}}{\text{percent}}$$

This set of equations can be used to solve percent word problems. All that is needed is to identify the part, whole, and/or percent, then to plug those values into the appropriate equation and solve.

PRACTICE QUESTIONS

33. Write 18% as a fraction.

34. Write $\frac{3}{5}$ as a percent.

35. Write 1.125 as a percent.

36. Write 84% as a decimal.

37. In a school of 650 students, 54% of the students are boys. How many students are girls?

PERCENT CHANGE

Percent change problems involve a change from an original amount. Often percent change problems appear as word problems that include discounts, growth, or markups. In order to solve percent change problems, it is necessary to identify the percent change (as a decimal), the amount of change, and the original amount. (Keep in mind that one of these will be the value being solved for.) These values can then be plugged into the equations below:

$$\text{amount of change} = \text{original amount} \times \text{percent change}$$

$$\text{percent change} = \frac{\text{amount of change}}{\text{original amount}}$$

$$\text{original amount} = \frac{\text{amount of change}}{\text{percent change}}$$

Comparison of Rational Numbers

Rational numbers can be ordered from least to greatest (or greatest to least) by placing them in the order in which they fall on a number line. When comparing a set of fractions, it is often easiest to convert each value to a common denominator. Then, it is only necessary to compare the numerators of each fraction.

When working with numbers in multiple forms (for example, a group of fractions and decimals), convert the values so that the set contains only fractions or only decimals. When ordering negative numbers, remember that the negative number with the largest absolute value is furthest from 0 and is therefore the smallest number. (For example, −75 is smaller than −25.)

Algebraic Expressions

The foundation of algebra is the **variable**, an unknown number represented by a symbol (usually a letter such as x or a). Variables can be preceded by a **coefficient**, which is a constant (i.e., a real number) in front of the variable, such as $4x$ or $-2a$. An **algebraic expression** is any sum, difference, product, or quotient of variables and numbers (for example $3x^2$, $2x + 7y - 1$, and $\frac{5}{x}$ are algebraic expressions). **Terms** are any quantities that are added or subtracted (for example, the terms of the expression $x^2 - 3x + 5$ are x^2, $3x$, and 5). A **polynomial expression** is an algebraic expression where all the exponents on the variables are whole numbers. A polynomial with two terms is known as a **binomial**, and one with three terms is a **trinomial**.

Operations with Expressions
ADDING AND SUBTRACTING

Expressions can be added or subtracted by simply adding and subtracting **like terms**, which are terms with the same variable part (the variables must be the same, with the same exponents on each variable). For example, in the expressions $2x + 3xy - 2z$ and

$6y + 2xy$, the like terms are $3xy$ and $2xy$. Adding the two expressions yields the new expression $2x + 5xy - 2z + 6y$. Note that the other terms did not change; they cannot combine because they have different variables.

PRACTICE QUESTION

43. If $a = 12x + 7xy - 9y$ and $b = 8x - 9xz + 7z$, what is $a + b$?

DISTRIBUTING AND FACTORING

Often, simplifying expressions requires distributing and factoring, which can be seen as two sides of the same coin. **Distribution** multiplies each term in the first factor by each term in the second factor to clear off parentheses, while **factoring** reverses this process, taking a polynomial in standard form and writing it as a product of two or more factors.

HELPFUL HINT
Operations with polynomials can always be checked by plugging the same value into both expressions.

When distributing a monomial through a polynomial, the expression outside the parentheses is multiplied by each term inside the parentheses. Remember, coefficients are multiplied and exponents are added, following the rules of exponents.

The first step in factoring a polynomial is always to "undistribute," or factor out, the greatest common factor (GCF) among the terms. The GCF is multiplied by, in parentheses, the expression that remains of each term when the GCF is divided out of each term. Factoring can be checked by multiplying the GCF factor through the parentheses again.

PRACTICE QUESTIONS

44. Expand the following expression: $5x(x^2 - 2c + 10)$

45. Expand the following expression: $x(5 + z) - z(4x - z^2)$

Linear Equations

An **equation** states that two expressions are equal to each other. Polynomial equations are categorized by the highest power of the variables they contain. For instance, the highest power of any exponent of a linear equation is 1, a quadratic equation has a variable raised to the second power, a cubic equation has a variable raised to the third power, and so on.

SOLVING LINEAR EQUATIONS

Solving an equation means finding the value(s) of the variable that make the equation true. To solve a linear equation, it is necessary to manipulate the terms so that the variable being solved for appears alone on exactly one side of the equal sign while everything else in the equation is on the other side.

HELPFUL HINT
On multiple-choice tests, you can avoid solving equations by just plugging the answer choices into the given equation to see which value makes the equation true.

The way to solve linear equations is to "undo" all the operations that connect numbers to the variable of interest. Follow these steps:

1. Eliminate fractions by multiplying each side by the least common multiple of any denominators.

2. Distribute to eliminate parentheses, braces, and brackets.

3. Combine like terms.

4. Use addition or subtraction to collect all terms containing the variable of interest to one side, and all terms not containing the variable to the other side.

5. Use multiplication or division to remove coefficients from the variable being solved for.

Sometimes there are no numeric values in the equation, or there will be a mix of numerous variables and constants. The goal will be to solve the equation for one of the variables in terms of the other variables. In this case, the answer will be an expression involving numbers and letters instead of a numeric value.

PRACTICE QUESTIONS

46. Solve for x: $(\frac{100(x+5)}{20}) = 1$.

47. Solve for x: $2(x+2)^2 - 2x^2 + 10 = 20$

GRAPHS OF LINEAR EQUATIONS

The most common way to write a linear equation is **slope-intercept form**:

$$y = mx + b$$

HELPFUL HINT

Use the phrase **begin, move** to remember that b is the y-intercept (where to begin) and m is the slope (how the line moves).

In this equation, m is the **slope**, and b is the **y-intercept**. Slope is often described as "rise over run" because it is calculated as the difference in y-values (rise) over the difference in x-values (run). The slope of the line is also the **rate of change** of the dependent variable y with respect to the independent variable x. The y-intercept is the point where the line crosses the y-axis, or where x equals zero.

To graph a linear equation, identify the y-intercept and place that point on the y-axis. Then, starting at the y-intercept, use the slope to count up (or down if negative) the "rise" part of the slope and to the right the "run" part of the slope to find a second point. These points can then be connected to draw the line. To find the equation of a line, identify the y-intercept, if possible, on the graph and use two easily identifiable points to find the slope.

PRACTICE QUESTIONS

48. What is the equation of the following line?

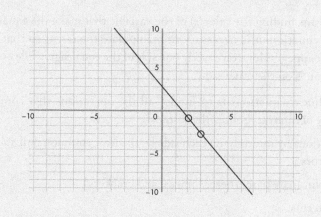

Building Equations

In word problems, it is often necessary to translate a verbal description of a relationship into a mathematical equation. No matter the problem, this process can be done using the same steps:

1. Read the problem carefully and identify what value needs to be solved for.
2. Identify the known and unknown quantities in the problem, and assign the unknown quantities a variable.
3. Create equations using the variables and known quantities.
4. Solve the equations.
5. Check the solution: Does it answer the question asked in the problem? Does it make sense?

HELPFUL HINT

Use the acronym **STAR** to remember word problem strategies. **S**earch the problem, **T**ranslate into an expression or equation, **A**nswer, and **R**eview.

PRACTICE QUESTIONS

50. A school is holding a raffle to raise money. There is a $3.00 entry fee, and each ticket costs $5.00. If a student paid $28.00, how many tickets did he buy?

51. Abby needs $395 to buy a new bicycle. She has borrowed $150 from her parents, and plans to earn the rest of the money working as a waitress. If she makes $10 per hour, how many hours will she need to work to pay for her new bicycle?

Inequalities

Inequalities are similar to equations, but both sides of the problem are not equal ($\neq$). Inequalities may be represented as follows: greater than ($>$), greater than or equal to ($\geq$), less than ($<$), or less than or equal to ($\leq$). For example, the statement "12 is less than 4 times x" would be written as $12 < 4x$.

Inequalities can be solved by manipulating them much like equations. However, the solution to an inequality is a set of numbers, not a single value. For example, simplifying $4x + 2 \leq 14$ gives the inequality $x \leq 3$, meaning every number less than 3 would also be included in the set of correct answers.

PRACTICE QUESTIONS

52. Solve the inequality: $4x + 10 > 58$

53. The students on the track team are buying new uniforms. T-shirts cost $12, pants cost $15, and a pair of shoes costs $45. If they have a budget of $2,500, write a mathematical sentence that represents how many of each item they can buy.

Units of Measurement

The standard units for the metric and American systems are shown below along with the prefixes used to express metric units.

Table 3.3. American and SI Units

Dimension	American	SI
Length	inch/foot/yard/mile	meter
Mass	ounce/pound/ton	gram
Volume	cup/pint/quart/gallon	liter
Force	pound-force	newton
Pressure	pound-force per square inch	pascal
Work and energy	cal/British thermal unit	joule
Temperature	Fahrenheit	kelvin
Charge	faraday	coulomb

Table 3.4. Metric Prefixes

Prefix	Symbol	Multiplication Factor
tera	T	1,000,000,000,000
giga	G	1,000,000,000
mega	M	1,000,000
kilo	k	1,000
hecto	h	100
deca	da	10
base unit	--	--
deci	d	0.1
centi	c	0.01
milli	m	0.001
micro	μ	0.000001
nano	n	0.000000001
pico	p	0.000000000001

Table 3.5. Conversion Factors

1 in. = 2.54 cm	1 lb. = 0.454 kg
1 yd. = 0.914 m	1 cal = 4.19 J
1 mi. = 1.61 km	$1°F = \frac{9}{5}°C + 32°C$
1 gal. = 3.785 L	$1 cm^3 = 1 mL$
1 oz. = 28.35 g	1 hr = 3600 s

HELPFUL HINT

A mnemonic device to help remember the metric system between kilo- and milli- is King Henry Drinks Under Dark Chocolate Moon (KHDUDCM).

Units can be converted within a single system or between systems. When converting from one unit to another unit, a **conversion factor** (a fraction used to convert a value with a unit into another unit) is used. For example, there are 2.54 centimeters in 1 inch, so the conversion factor from inches to centimeters is $\frac{2.54 \text{ centimeters}}{1 \text{ inch}}$.

To convert between units, multiply the original value by a conversion factor (or several if needed) so that the original units cancel, leaving the desired unit. Remember that the original value can be made into a fraction by placing it over 1.

$$\frac{3 \text{ inches}}{1} \times \frac{2.54 \text{ centimeters}}{1 \text{ inch}} = 7.62 \text{ centimeters}$$

Units can be canceled (meaning they disappear from the expression) when they appear on the top and the bottom of a fraction. If the same unit appears in the top (or bottom) of both fractions, you probably need to flip the conversion factor.

PRACTICE QUESTIONS

54. Convert 4.25 kilometers to meters.

55. Convert 12 feet to inches.

Geometric Figures

CLASSIFYING GEOMETRIC FIGURES

Geometric figures are shapes comprised of points, lines, or planes. A **point** is simply a location in space; it does not have any dimensional properties like length, area, or volume. A collection of points that extend infinitely in both directions is a **line**, and one that extends infinitely in only one direction is a **ray**. A section of a line with a beginning and end point is a **line segment**. Lines, rays, and line segments are examples of **one-dimensional** objects because they can only be measured in one dimension (length).

Figure 3.4. One-Dimensional Object

Lines, rays, and line segments can intersect to create **angles**, which are measured in degrees or radians. Angles between zero and 90 degrees are **acute**, and angles between 90 and 180 degrees are **obtuse**. An angle of exactly 90 degrees is a **right angle**, and two lines that form right angles are **perpendicular**. Lines that do not intersect are described as **parallel**.

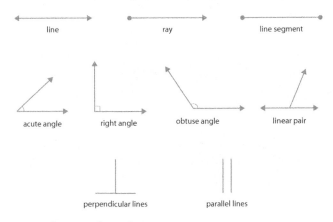

Figure 3.5A. Lines and Angles

perpendicular lines   parallel lines

Figure 3.5B. Lines and Angles

Figure 3.6. Two-Dimensional Object

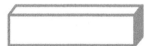

Figure 3.7. Three-Dimensional Object

Figure 3.5B. Lines and Angles

Two-dimensional objects can be measured in two dimensions—length and width. A **plane** is a two-dimensional object that extends infinitely in both directions. **Polygons** are two-dimensional shapes, such as triangles and squares, which have three or more straight sides. Regular polygons are polygons whose sides are all the same length.

Three-dimensional objects, such as cubes, can be measured in three dimensions—length, width, and height.

CALCULATING GEOMETRIC QUANTITIES

The **length**, or distance from one point to another on an object, can be determined using a tape measure or a ruler. The size of the surface of a two-dimensional object is its **area**. Generally, finding area involves multiplying one dimension of an object by another, such as length by width. For example, if a window is 3 feet long and 2 feet wide, its area would be 6 ft².

The distance around a two-dimensional figure is its **perimeter**, which can be found by adding the lengths of all the sides. The distance around a circle is referred to as its **circumference**.

Table 3.6. Area and Perimeter of Basic Shapes

Shape	Example	Area	Perimeter
Triangle	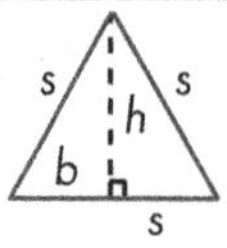	$A = \frac{1}{2} bh$	$P = s_1 + s_2 + s_3$
Square	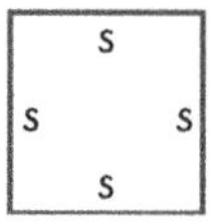	$A = s^2$	$P = 4s$

Shape	Example	Area	Perimeter
Rectangle		$A = l \times w$	$P = 2l + 2w$
Trapezoid		$A = \frac{1}{2}h(b_1 + b_2)$	$P = b_1 + b_2 + l_1 + l_2$
Circle		$A = \pi r^2$	$C = 2\pi r$
Sector		$A = \frac{x°}{360°}(\pi r^2)$	arc length $= \frac{x°}{360°}(2\pi r)$

For the rectangle below, the area would be 8 m² because 2 m × 4 m = 8 m². The perimeter of the rectangle would be $P = 2l + 2w = 2(4 \text{ m}) + 2(2 \text{ m}) = 12 \text{ m}$.

The **surface area** of a three-dimensional object can be figured by adding the areas of all the sides. For example, the box below is 4 feet long, 3 feet wide, and 1 foot deep. The surface area is found by adding the areas of each face:

- top: 4 ft × 3 ft = 12 ft²
- bottom: 4 ft × 3 ft = 12 ft²
- front: 4 ft × 1 ft = 4 ft²
- back: 4 ft × 1 ft = 4 ft²
- right: 1 ft × 3 ft = 3 ft²
- left: 1 ft × 3 ft = 3 ft²

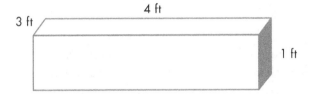

Figure 3.8. Surface Area

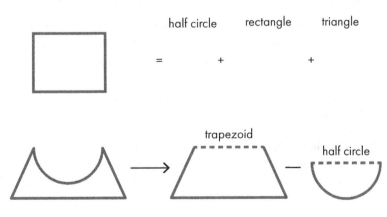

Figure 3.9. Compound Shapes

The KNAT may also ask test takers to find the perimeter and area of compound shapes, which will include parts of circles, squares, triangles, or other polygons joined together to create an irregular shape. For these types of problems, the first step is to divide the figure into shapes whose area (or perimeter) can easily be solved for. Then, solve each part separately and add (or subtract) the parts together for the final answer.

PRACTICE QUESTIONS

56. What is the area of the figure shown below?

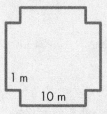

57. What is the area of the shaded region in the figure below?

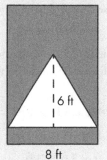

Statistics

Statistics is the study of data. Analyzing data requires using **measures of central tendency** (mean, median, and mode) to identify trends or patterns.

The **mean** is the average; it is determined by adding all outcomes and then dividing by the total number of outcomes. For example, the average of the data set {16, 19, 19, 25, 27, 29, 75} is equal to $\frac{16 + 19 + 19 + 25 + 27 + 29 + 75}{7} = \frac{210}{7} = 30$.

The **median** is the number in the middle when the data set is arranged in order from least to greatest. For example, in the data set {16, 19, 19, **25**, 27, 29, 75}, the median is 25. When a data set contains an even number of values, finding the median requires averaging the two middle values. In the data set {75, 80, 82, 100}, the two numbers in the middle are 80 and 82. Consequently, the median will be the average of these two values: $\frac{80 + 82}{2} = 81$.

Finally, the **mode** is the most frequent outcome in a data set. In the set {16, 19, 19, 25, 27, 29, 75}, the mode is 19 because it occurs twice, which is more than any of the other numbers. If several values appear an equal, and most frequent, number of times, both values are considered the mode. If every value in a data set appears only once, the data set has no mode.

Other useful indicators include range and outliers. The **range** is the difference between the highest and the lowest values in a data set. For example, the range of the set {16, 19, 19, 25, 27, 29, 75} is 75 − 16 = 59.

Outliers, or data points that are much different from other data points, should be noted as they can skew the central tendency. In the data set {16, 19, 19, 25, 27, 29, 75}, the value 75 is far outside the other values and raises the value of the mean. Without the outlier, the mean is much closer to the other data points.

- $$\frac{16 + 19 + 19 + 25 + 27 + 29 + 75}{7} = \frac{210}{7} = 30$$

- $$\frac{16 + 19 + 19 + 25 + 27 + 29}{6} = \frac{135}{6} = 22.5$$

Generally, the median is a better indicator of a central tendency if outliers are present to skew the mean.

Trends in a data set can also be seen by graphing the data as a dot plot. The distribution of the data can then be described based on the shape of the graph. A **symmetric** distribution looks like two mirrored halves, while a **skewed** distribution is weighted more heavily toward the right or the left. Note the direction of the skew describes the side of the graph with fewer data points. In a **uniform** data set, the points are distributed evenly along the graph.

A symmetric or skewed distribution may have peaks, or sets of data points that appear more frequently. A **unimodal** distribution has one peak while a **bimodal** distribution has two peaks. A normal (or bell-shaped) distribution is a special symmetric, unimodal graph with a specific distribution of data points.

PRACTICE QUESTIONS

58. Which of the following best describes the distribution of the graph?

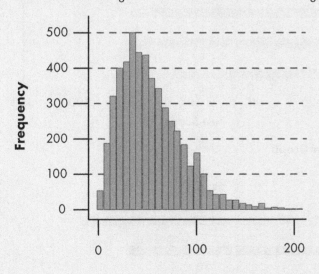

A) skewed left

B) skewed right

C) bimodal

D) uniform

59. Which of the following is the mean of the data set?

14, 18, 11, 28, 23, 14

A) 11

B) 14

C) 18

D) 28

Data Presentation

Data can be presented in a variety of ways. In addition to a simple table, there are a number of different graphs and charts that can be used to visually represent data. The most appropriate type of graph or chart depends on the data being displayed.

Box plots (also called box and whisker plots) show data using the median, range, and outliers of a data set. They provide a helpful visual guide, showing how data is distributed around the median. In the example below, 70 is the median and the range is 0 – 100, or 100.

Figure 3.10. Box Plot

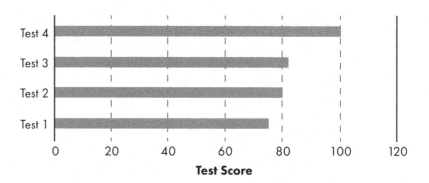

Figure 3.11. Bar Graph

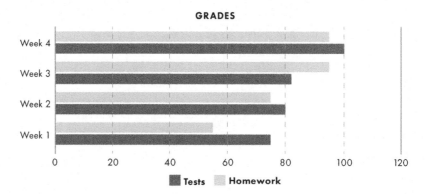

Figure 3.12. Double Bar Graph

Bar graphs use bars of different lengths to compare data. The independent variable on a bar graph is grouped into categories such as months, flavors, or locations, and the dependent variable is a quantity. Thus, comparing the length of bars provides a visual guide to the relative amounts in each category. **Double bar graphs** show more than one data set on the same set of axes.

Histograms similarly use bars to compare data, but the independent variable is a continuous variable that has been "binned" or divided into categories. For example, the time of day can be broken down into 8:00 a.m. to 12:00 p.m., 12:00 p.m. to 4:00 p.m., and so on. Usually (but not always), a gap is included between the bars of a bar graph but not a histogram. The bars of a bar graph show actual data, but the bars (or bins) of a histogram show the frequency of the data in various ranges.

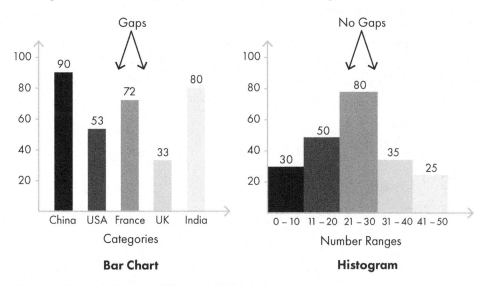

Figure 3.13. Bar Chart vs. Histogram

Dot plots display the frequency of a value or event data graphically using dots, and thus can be used to observe the distribution of a data set. Typically, a value or category is listed on the x-axis, and the number of times that value appears in the data set is represented by a line of vertical dots. Dot plots make it easy to see which values occur most often.

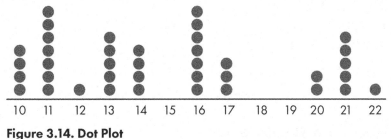

Figure 3.14. Dot Plot

Scatter plots use points to show relationships between two variables which can be plotted as coordinate points. One variable describes a position on the x-axis, and the other a point on the y-axis. Scatter plots can suggest relationships between variables. For example, both variables might increase together, or one may increase when the other decreases.

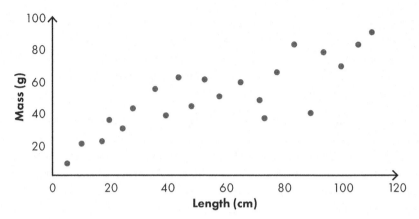

Figure 3.15. Scatter Plot

Line graphs show changes in data by connecting points on a scatter graph using a line. These graphs will often measure time on the *x*-axis and are used to show trends in the data, such as temperature changes over a day or school attendance throughout the year. **Double line graphs** present two sets of data on the same set of axes.

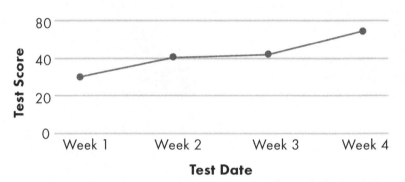

Figure 3.16. Line Graph

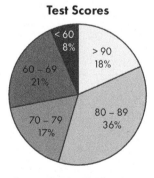

Figure 3.18. Circle Graph

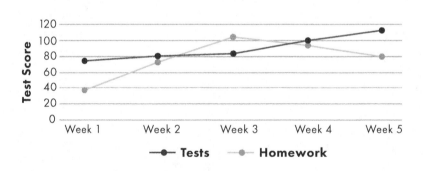

Figure 3.17. Double Line Graph

Circle graphs (also called pie charts) are used to show parts of a whole: the "pie" is the whole, and each "slice" represents a percentage or part of the whole.

PRACTICE QUESTION

60. Students are asked if they prefer vanilla, chocolate, or strawberry ice cream. The results are tallied on the following table.

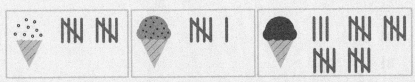

Four students display the information from the table in a bar graph. Which student completes the bar graph correctly?

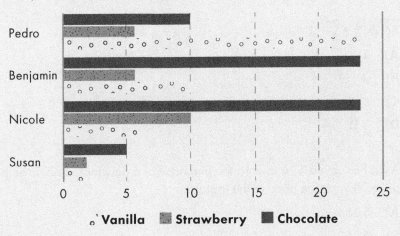

A) Pedro

B) Benjamin

C) Nicole

D) Susan

Mathematics Review Questions

1. Simplify the following expression:
   $$\frac{4x^6y^2}{3x^2y^4}$$
   - **A)** x^3y^2
   - **B)** $\frac{4x^3}{y^2}$
   - **C)** $\frac{4x^4}{3y^2}$
   - **D)** $12x^4y^2$

2. Solve: $\frac{x}{3} + \frac{7}{6} = \frac{5}{2}$
   - **A)** 11
   - **B)** 4
   - **C)** 0
   - **D)** -11

3. Asha has saved $96 toward the purchase of a new laptop, 20% of its price. What is the price of the laptop?
   - **A)** $864
   - **B)** $960
   - **C)** $380
   - **D)** $480

4. Solve: $6x - 7 = 5(2x + 1)$
   - **A)** -3
   - **B)** -2
   - **C)** 4
   - **D)** 3

5. Two units of a certain gas weigh 175 grams. What is the weight of 5 units of this gas?
   - **A)** 70 g
   - **B)** 875 g
   - **C)** 1750 g
   - **D)** 437.5 g

6. Convert $\frac{2}{3}$ to a decimal number. Round the answer to the nearest hundredth.
   - **A)** 0.6
   - **B)** 0.67

C) 0.66

D) 0.7

7. If three lengths of copper wire, $6\frac{2}{5}$ feet each, are cut off a 100-foot roll of copper wire, how much wire is left on the roll?

A) $19\frac{1}{5}$ ft

B) $93\frac{3}{5}$ ft

C) $80\frac{4}{5}$ ft

D) $81\frac{1}{5}$ ft

8. A particular baseball statistic, OPS, is the sum of a batter's on-base percentage and slugging percentage. Find the OPS for a player with an on-base percentage of 0.308 and a slugging percentage of 0.486.

A) 0.794

B) 0.178

C) 0.150

D) 0.397

9. Simplify the following expression:

$15 \div 3 \times 5 - 10$

A) −15

B) −9

C) −25

D) 15

10. An emergency surgery begins at 2300 hours. The surgery is expected to last 3 hours. At what time is the surgery likely to end?

A) 0300

B) 0200

C) 2600

D) 1400

11. Convert 6.5 feet to meters. Round the answer to the nearest hundredth.

A) 1.98 m

B) 198 m

C) 78 m

D) 7.8 m

12. Simplify the following expression:

$3xy(x^2 - 11xy + 10y^2)$

A) $3x^4y^4$

B) $3x^3y - 33x^2y^2 + 30xy^3$

C) $3x^3y - 11xy + 10y^2$

D) $3x^3y + 33x^2y^2 - 30xy^3$

13. There were 135 people in an auditorium. If the auditorium was 45% full, how many seats are in the auditorium?

A) 300 seats

B) 608 seats

C) 180 seats

D) 500 seats

14. Simplify the following expression:

$\dfrac{10x^9y^6}{5x^3y^2}$

A) $2x^6y^4$

B) $2x^3y^3$

C) $5x^3y^3$

D) $5xy$

15. Solve: $\dfrac{x}{4} + \dfrac{2}{3} = \dfrac{29}{12}$

A) 5

B) 12

C) 7

D) 10

16. If property taxes are figured at \$1.50 for every \$100 in evaluation, what taxes will be paid on a home valued at \$85,000?

A) \$567

B) \$12,750

C) \$1275

D) \$5670

17. Find the product of $\dfrac{10}{21}$ and $\dfrac{14}{25}$.

A) $\dfrac{125}{147}$

B) $\dfrac{12}{23}$

C) 1

D) $\frac{4}{15}$

18. 8.653 + 2 + 1.06 =

A) 8.761

B) 11.713

C) 9.715

D) 9.913

19. A patient enters the emergency room at 11:15 a.m. The patient is discharged 4 hours later. Express the time the patient left the ER in military time.

A) 1515

B) 0315

C) 0515

D) 0715

20. A snail moves about 0.029 miles per hour. Convert its speed to inches per second.

A) 0.23 in/sec

B) 0.51 in/sec

C) 5 in/sec

D) 2 in/sec

21. Simplify the following expression:

$4x - 3(y - 2x)$

A) $2x - 3y$

B) $-2x + 3y$

C) $3y - 10x$

D) $10x - 3y$

22. Chan owes his parents $2500. So far he has paid back $800. What percent of the original loan has Chan paid back?

A) 68%

B) 32%

C) 16%

D) 8%

23. Simplify the following expression:

$$\frac{9\,a^7 b^3}{18\,a^2 b^5}$$

A) $2a^5 b^2$

B) $\frac{a^5}{9\,b^2}$

C) $\frac{a^5}{2\,b^2}$

D) $2a^9 b^8$

24. Solve the following proportion:

$$\frac{25}{100} = \frac{12}{x}$$

A) 48

B) 3

C) 1200

D) 300

25. A recipe calls for $1\frac{3}{4}$ cups sugar. How much sugar is needed to triple the recipe?

A) $3\frac{3}{4}$ c

B) $\frac{7}{12}$ c

C) $5\frac{1}{4}$ c

D) $4\frac{1}{5}$ c

26. Simplify the following expression:

$6a^3 b^2(5a^2 b^5 c)$

A) $11a^5 b^7 c$

B) $30ab^2 c$

C) $30a^6 b^{10} c$

D) $30a^5 b^7 c$

27. Eduardo has made $24\frac{1}{2}$ ounces of homemade tomato sauce. How many $3\frac{1}{2}$-ounce jars can he fill?

A) 7 jars

B) 8 jars

C) 12 jars

D) 6 jars

28. Find 9% of 81.

    A) 9

    B) 7.29

    C) 90

    D) 72

29. An investor believes she will make $12 for every $100 she invests. How much would she expect to make on a $1500 investment?

    A) $125

    B) $112

    C) $180

    D) $120

30. 65 − 14.46 + 5.8 =

    A) 14.53

    B) 15.69

    C) 56.34

    D) 73.66

31. A pregnant woman arrives at the hospital at 1:00 p.m. After five and a half hours, she delivers a healthy baby boy. What time of birth will be recorded in the chart?

    A) 0630

    B) 1230

    C) 1630

    D) 1830

32. If $285.48 will be shared equally by six people, how much will each person receive?

    A) $1712.88

    B) $47.58

    C) $885.46

    D) $225.48

33. The distance from Boston to New York City is 215 miles. Convert the distance to kilometers. Round to the nearest whole number.

    A) 108 km

    B) 134 km

    C) 400 km

    D) 346 km

34. Simplify the following expression:

$2(3x + 4y) + 7(2x - 2y)$

A) $20x - 6y$

B) $5x + 2y$

C) $20x^2 - 6y^2$

D) $20x + 22y$

35. Sarah works $22\frac{1}{2}$ hours per week, which she splits between two departments. Sarah spends $\frac{1}{3}$ of her hours working for the marketing department. How many hours per week does Sarah work for marketing?

A) $6\frac{1}{3}$ hr

B) 7 hr

C) $7\frac{1}{2}$ hr

D) $8\frac{2}{3}$ hr

36. Find 90% of 62.

A) 55.8

B) 7.2

C) 5.58

D) 0.72

37. Solve the proportion:

$\frac{3.5}{2.6} = \frac{10.5}{x}$

A) 27.3

B) 7.8

C) 36.75

D) 14.1

38. How many $\frac{1}{3}$-cup servings can be poured from $5\frac{2}{3}$ cups juice?

A) 17 servings

B) $1\frac{1}{9}$ servings

C) 51 servings

D) $15\frac{1}{3}$ servings

39. What is the price of 2.7 pounds of steak at $5.40 per pound?

  A) $16.20

  B) $8.10

  C) $13.50

  D) $14.58

40. 140 is 35% of what number?

  A) 260

  B) 400

  C) 175

  D) 500

41. The ratio of teachers to students at Smith Community College is 2 to 19. If the enrollment at the college is 2014 students, how many teachers are there?

  A) 191 teachers

  B) 53 teachers

  C) 106 teachers

  D) 212 teachers

42. $7\frac{1}{3} \div \frac{4}{5} =$

  A) $9\frac{1}{6}$

  B) $5\frac{13}{15}$

  C) $\frac{6}{55}$

  D) $\frac{15}{88}$

43. Find the product of 6.2 and 8.5.

  A) 527

  B) 14.7

  C) 52.7

  D) 2.3

44. 88 is what percent of 160?

  A) 72%

  B) 55%

  C) 2.2%

  D) 22%

45. An employee is given $100 petty cash to purchase 6 binders and 6 sets of dividers at the office supply store. Divider sets are $3.49 each, and the binders come in packages of two for $10.49 per package. How much money will the employee return to petty cash?

   A) $52.41
   B) $16.12
   C) $83.88
   D) $47.59

46. Marcus works maintenance for a large apartment complex. He averages $\frac{2}{3}$ hour per maintenance call. How many calls can he take in an 8-hour work day?

   A) 6 calls
   B) 12 calls
   C) 24 calls
   D) 36 calls

47. The cost of 2.4 yards of lumber is $24.96. What is the cost per yard?

   A) $5.99
   B) $10.40
   C) $22.46
   D) $27.36

48. The price of a movie ticket increased from $9.75 to $11.50. Find the percent increase. Round your answer to the nearest tenth of a percent.

   A) 84.8%
   B) 22%
   C) 17.9%
   D) 15.2%

49. How many $1\frac{1}{3}$-pound loaves of bread can be made from 8 pounds of dough?

   A) $3\frac{2}{3}$ loaves
   B) 12 loaves
   C) 6 loaves
   D) $6\frac{2}{3}$ loaves

50. Find the batting average of a baseball player who get 14 hits in 52 at-bats. (Divide the number of hits by the number of at-bats. Round to the nearest thousandth.)

A) 0.145

B) 3.714

C) 0.269

D) 0.380

1.   **Natural**, **whole**, **integer**, and **rational** (72 can be written as the fraction $\frac{72}{1}$).

2.   **Rational** (The number is a fraction.)

3.   **Irrational** (The number cannot be written as a fraction, and written as a decimal it is approximately 2.2360679... Notice this decimal does not terminate, nor does it have a repeating pattern.)

4.   In order to add, the exponents of 10 must be the same. Change the first number so the power of 10 is 2:

$3.8 \times 10^3 = 3.8 \times 10 \times 10^2 = 38 \times 10^2$

Add the terms together and write the number in proper scientific notation:

$38 \times 10^2 + 4.7 \times 10^2 = 42.7 \times 10^2 = \mathbf{4.27 \times 10^3}$

5.   Multiply the factors and add the exponents on the base of 10:

$(8.1 \times 1.4)(10^{-5} \times 10^7) = 11.34 \times 10^2$

Write the number in proper scientific notation: (Place the decimal so that the first number is between 1 and 10 and adjust the exponent accordingly.)

$11.34 \times 10^2 = \mathbf{1.134 \times 10^3}$

6.   Since $|-18| > |12|$, the answer is negative. $|-18| - |12| = 6$. So the answer is **−6**.

7.   Adding two negative numbers results in a negative number. Add the values: **−5.82**

8.   **5.12**

9.   Change the subtraction to addition, change the sign of the second number, then add:

$86 - (-20) = 86 + (+20) = \mathbf{106}$

10.   Multiply the numerators, multiply the denominators, then simplify: $-\frac{90}{15} = \mathbf{-6}$

11.   A negative divided by a negative is a positive number: **6.4**

12.   The parentheses indicate multiplication: **7.26**

13.   A negative divided by a positive is negative: **−4**

14.   Calculate the expressions inside the parenthesis:

$2(21 - 14) + 6 \div (-2) \times 3 - 10 =$

$2(7) + 6 \div (-2) \times 3 - 10$

There are no exponents or radicals, so perform multiplication and division from left to right:

$2(7) + 6 \div (-2) \times 3 - 10 =$

$14 + 6 \div (-2) \times 3 - 10 =$

$14 + (-3) \times 3 - 10 =$

$14 + (-9) - 10$

Lastly, perform addition and subtraction from left to right:

$14 + (-9) - 10 = 5 - 10 = \mathbf{-5}$

15. Calculate the expressions inside the parentheses:

$-(3)^2 + 4(5) + (5-6)^2 - 8 =$

$-(3)^2 + 4(5) + (-1)^2 - 8$

Simplify exponents and radicals:

$-(3)^2 + 4(5) + (-1)^2 - 8 =$

$-9 + 4(5) + 1 - 8$

Note that $-(3)^2 = -1(3)^2 = -9$ but $(-1)^2 = (-1)(-1) = 1$

Perform multiplication and division from left to right:

$-9 + 4(5) + 1 - 8 =$

$-9 + 20 + 1 - 8$

Lastly, perform addition and subtraction from left to right:

$-9 + 20 + 1 - 8 =$

$11 + 1 - 8 = 12 - 8 = \mathbf{4}$

16. Simplify the top and bottom expressions separately using the same steps described above:

$$\frac{(-2)^3 + 8(-2)}{4^2 - 5^2} = \frac{-8 + (-16)}{16 - 25} = \frac{-24}{-9} = \mathbf{\frac{8}{3}}$$

17. Apply the order of operations left to right:

$24.38 + 16.51 = 40.89$

$40.89 - 29.87 = \mathbf{11.02}$

18. Multiply the numbers ignoring the decimals: $104 \times 182 = 18{,}928$

The original problem includes two decimal places (10.4 has one place after the decimal point and 18.2 has one place after the decimal point), so place the decimal point in the answer so that there are two places after the decimal point. Estimating is a good way to check the answer ($10.4 \approx 10$, $18.2 \approx 18$, $10 \times 18 = 180$)

$18{,}928 \rightarrow \mathbf{189.28}$

19. The divisor is 2.5. Move the decimal one place to the right (multiply 2.5 by 10) so that the divisor is a whole number. Since the decimal point of the divisor was moved one place to the right, the decimal point in the dividend must be moved one place to the right (multiplying it by 10 as well).

$80 \rightarrow 800$ and $2.5 \rightarrow 25$

Divide normally: $800 \div 25 = \mathbf{32}$

20. The first step is to change each fraction so it has a denominator of 20, which is the LCD of 5, 4, and 2:

$$2\frac{3}{5} + 3\frac{1}{4} - 1\frac{1}{2} = 2\frac{12}{20} + 3\frac{5}{20} - 1\frac{10}{20}$$

Next, add and subtract the whole numbers together and the fractions together:

$2 + 3 - 1 = 4$

$\frac{12}{20} + \frac{5}{20} - \frac{10}{20} = \frac{7}{20}$

Lastly, combine to get the final answer (a mixed number): $\mathbf{4\frac{7}{20}}$

21. Change the mixed number to an improper fraction: $3\frac{1}{3} = \frac{10}{3}$

Multiply the numerators together and the denominators together, and then reduce the fraction:

$$\frac{7}{8}\left(\frac{10}{3}\right) = \frac{7 \times 10}{8 \times 3} = \frac{70}{24} = \frac{35}{12} = \mathbf{2\frac{11}{12}}$$

22. Change the mixed number to an improper fraction. Then, multiply the first fraction by the reciprocal of the second fraction and simplify:

$$\frac{9}{2} \div \frac{2}{3} = \frac{9}{2} \times \frac{3}{2} = \frac{27}{4} = \mathbf{6\frac{3}{4}}$$

23. Divide the denominator into the numerator using long division:

```
      0.875
  8 ⟌ 7.0000
     -64 ↓
       60
      -56 ↓
        60
       -56 ↓
         40
        -40
          0
```

24. Dividing using long division yields a repeating decimal:

```
       0.4545
  11 ⟌ 5.0000
      -4 4 ↓
         60
        -55 ↓
         50
        -44 ↓
          60
         -55
           5
```

25. Place the numbers to the right of the decimal (125) in the numerator. There are three numbers, so put the number 1000 in the denominator, and then reduce: $\frac{125}{1000} = \mathbf{\frac{1}{8}}$

26. The 8 is in the thousands place, and the number to its right is a 4. Because 4 is less than 5, the 8 remains and all numbers to the right become zero:

$$138,472 \approx \mathbf{138,000}$$

27. Round each value to the thousands place and add:

$12,341 \approx 12,000$

$8,975 \approx 9,000$

$9,431 \approx 9,000$

$10,521 \approx 11,000$

$11,427 \approx 11,000$

$12,000 + 9,000 + 9,000 + 11,000 + 11,000 = \mathbf{52,000}$

28. There are 22 total students in the class. The ratio can be written as $\frac{10}{22}$, and reduced to $\frac{5}{11}$. The ratio of girls to boys is **12:10 or 6:5**.

29. The family's total expenses for the month add up to $2,300. The ratio of the rent to total amount of expenses can be written as $\frac{600}{2300}$ and reduced to $\frac{6}{23}$.

30. Start by cross multiplying:

$\frac{3-5}{2} = \frac{-8}{3} \rightarrow 3(3-5x) = 2(-8)$

Then, solve the equation:

$9 - 15x = -16$

$-15x = -25$

$x = \frac{-25}{-15} = \frac{5}{3}$

31. Write a proportion where x equals the actual distance and each ratio is written as inches:miles.

$\frac{2.5}{40} = \frac{17.25}{x}$

Then, cross-multiply and divide to solve: $2.5x = 690$

$x = 276$

The two cities are 276 miles apart.

32. Write a proportion in which x is the number of defective parts made and both ratios are written as defective parts:total parts.

$\frac{4}{1000} = \frac{x}{125,000}$

Then, cross-multiply and divide to solve for x: $1000x = 500,000$

$x = 500$

There are 500 defective parts for the month.

33. The percent is written as a fraction over 100 and reduced: $\frac{18}{100} = \frac{9}{50}$

34. Dividing 5 by 3 gives the value 0.6, which is then multiplied by 100: **60%**.

35. The decimal point is moved two places to the right: **112.5%**.

36. The decimal point is moved two places to the left: 84% = **0.84**.

37. The first step is to find the percent of students who are girls by subtracting from 100%: $100\% - 54\% = 46\%$

Next, identify the variables and plug into the appropriate equation:

percent = 46% = 0.46

whole = 650 students

part = ?

part = whole × percent = 0.46 × 650 = 299

There are 299 girls.

38. The first step is to identify the necessary values. These can then be plugged into the appropriate equation:

original amount = 1,500

percent change = 45% = 0.45

amount of change = ?

amount of change = original amount × percent change = 1,500 × 0.45 = 675

To find the new price, subtract the amount of change from the original price:
1,500 − 675 = 825 → The final price is **$825**.

39. Identify the necessary values and plug into the appropriate equation:

original amount = 100,000

amount of change = 120,000 − 100,000 = 20,000

percent change = ?

$$\text{percent change} = \frac{\text{amount of change}}{\text{original amount}}$$

$$= \frac{20,000}{100,000} = 0.20$$

To find the percent growth, multiply by 100: 0.20 × 100 = **20%**

40. Change each fraction to a decimal:

$$-\frac{2}{3} = -0.\overline{66}$$

$$\frac{5}{4} = 1.25$$

$$\frac{1}{8} = 0.125$$

Now place the decimals in order from greatest to least:

1.25, 1.2, 0.125, 0, −0.$\overline{66}$, −1, −2.1

Lastly, convert back to fractions if the problem requires it:

$\frac{5}{4}$, 1.2, $\frac{1}{8}$, 0, −$\frac{2}{3}$, −1, −2.1

41. Convert each value using the least common denominator value of 24:

$$\frac{1}{3} = \frac{8}{24}$$

$$-\frac{5}{6} = -\frac{20}{24}$$

$$1\frac{1}{8} = \frac{9}{8} = \frac{27}{24}$$

$$\frac{7}{12} = \frac{14}{24}$$

$$-\frac{3}{4} = -\frac{18}{24}$$

$$-\frac{3}{2} = -\frac{36}{24}$$

Next, put the fractions in order from least to greatest by comparing the numerators:

$-\frac{36}{24}$, $-\frac{20}{24}$, $-\frac{18}{24}$, $\frac{8}{24}$, $\frac{14}{24}$, $\frac{27}{24}$

Finally, put the fractions back in their original form if the problem requires it:

$-\frac{3}{2}$, $-\frac{5}{6}$, $-\frac{3}{4}$, $\frac{1}{3}$, $\frac{7}{12}$, $1\frac{1}{8}$

42. First, plug the value 4 in for m in the expression:

$$5(m − 2)^3 + 3m^2 − \frac{m}{4} − 1$$

$$= 5(4 − 2)^3 + 3(4)^2 − \frac{4}{4} − 1$$

Then, simplify using PEMDAS:

P: $5(2)^3 + 3(4)^2 − \frac{4}{4} − 1$

E: $5(8) + 3(16) − \frac{4}{4} − 1$

M and D, working left to right: 40 + 48 − 1 − 1

A and S, working left to right: **86**

43. The only like terms in both expressions are $12x$ and $8x$, so these two terms will be added, and all other terms will remain the same:

$a + b = (12x + 8x) + 7xy - 9y - 9xz + 7z$

$= 20x + 7xy - 9y - 9xz + 7z$

44. The term outside the parentheses must be distributed and multiplied by all three terms inside the parentheses:

$(5x)(x^2) = 5x^3$

$(5x)(-2c) = -10xc$

$(5x)(10) = 50x$

$5x(x^2 - 2c + 10) \rightarrow$ **$5x^3 - 10xc + 50x$**

45. Start by distributing for each set of parentheses:

$x(5 + z) - z(4x - z^2)$

Notice that $-z$ is distributed and that $(-z)(-z^2) = +z^3$. Failing to distribute the negative is a very common error.

$5x + xz - 4zx + z^3$

Note that xz is a like term with zx (commutative property), and they can therefore be combined.

Now combine like terms and place terms in the appropriate order (highest exponents first): **$z^3 - 3xz + 5x$**

46. To cancel out the denominator, multiply both sides by 20:

$20 \dfrac{100(x + 5)}{20} = 1 \times 20$

$100(x + 5) = 20$

Next, distribute 100 through the parentheses:

$100(x + 5) = 20$

$100x + 500 = 20$

"Undo" the +500 by subtracting 500 from both sides of the equation to isolate the variable term: $100x = -480$

Finally, "undo" the multiplication by 100: divide by 100 on both sides to solve for x:

$x = \dfrac{-480}{100} = -4.8$

47. First, simplify the left-hand side of the equation using order of operations and combining like terms.

$2(x + 2)^2 - 2x^2 + 10 = 20$

Do the exponent first: $2(x + 2)(x + 2) - 2x^2 + 10 = 20$

FOIL: $2(x^2 + 4x + 4) - 2x^2 + 10 = 20$

Distribute the 2: $2x^2 + 8x + 8 - 2x^2 + 10 = 20$

Combine like terms on the left-hand side: $8x + 18 = 20$

Now, isolate the variable.

"Undo" +18 by subtracting 18 from both sides: $8x + 18 = 20$

$8x = 2$

"Undo" multiplication by 8 by dividing both sides by 8: **$x = \dfrac{2}{8}$ or $\dfrac{1}{4}$**

48. The y-intercept can be identified on the graph as $(0, 3)$. Thus, $b = 3$.

To find the slope, choose any two points and plug the values into the slope equation. The two points chosen here are $(2, -1)$ and $(3, -3)$.

$$m = \frac{(-3) - (-1)}{3 - 2} = \frac{-2}{1} = -2$$

Replace m with -2 and b with 3 in $y = mx + b$.

The equation of the line is **$y = -2x + 3$**.

49. Rearrange the equation into slope-intercept form by solving the equation for y. Isolate $-2y$ by subtracting $6x$ and adding 8 to both sides of the equation.

$-2y = -6x + 8$

Divide both sides by -2:

$$y = \frac{-6x + 8}{-2}$$

Simplify the fraction.

$y = 3x - 4$

The slope is 3, since it is the coefficient of x.

50. The problem is asking for the number of tickets. First, identify the quantities:

number of tickets = x

cost per ticket = 5

cost for x tickets = $5x$

total cost = 28

entry fee = 3

Now, set up an equation. The total cost for x tickets will be equal to the cost for x tickets plus the \$3 entry fee: $5x + 3 = 28$

Now solve the equation:

$5x + 3 = 28$

$5x = 25$

$x = 5$

The student bought 5 tickets.

51. The problem asks for the number of hours Abby will have to work. First, identify the quantities:

number of hours = x

amount earned per hour = 10

amount of money earned = $10x$

price of bicycle = 395

money borrowed = 150

Now, set up an equation. The amount of money she has borrowed plus the money she earned as a waitress needs to equal the cost of the bicycle: $10x + 150 = 395$

Now solve the equation:

$10x + 150 = 395$

$10x = 245$

$x = 24.5$ hours

She will need to work 24.5 hours.

52. Inequalities can be solved using the same steps used to solve equations. Start by subtracting 10 from both sides:

$4x + 10 > 58$

$4x > 48$

Now divide by 4 to isolate x: **$x > 12$**

53. They have to spend less than $2,500 on uniforms, so this problem is an inequality. First, identify the quantities:

number of t-shirts = t

total cost of t-shirts = $12t$

number of pants = p

total cost of pants = $15p$

number of pairs of shoes = s

total cost of shoes = $45s$

The cost of all the items must be less than $2,500: **$12t + 15p + 45s < 2,500$**

54. $4.25 \text{ km}(\frac{1000 \text{ m}}{1 \text{ km}}) =$ **4250 m**

55. $12 \text{ ft}(\frac{12 \text{ in}}{1 \text{ ft}}) =$ **144 in**

56. The figure can be broken apart into three rectangles:

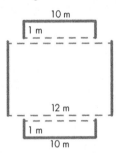

The area of each smaller rectangle is 1 m × 10 m = 10 m². The area of the larger rectangle is 10 m × 12 m = 120 m². Together, the area of the three shapes is 10 m² + 10 m² + 120 m² = **140 m²**

57. The area of the shaded region is the area of the rectangle minus the area of the triangle:

rectangle − triangle = (8 ft × 16 ft) − (0.5 × 8 ft × 6 ft) = 128 ft² − 24 ft² = **104 ft²**

58. **B) is correct.** The graph is skewed right because there are fewer data points on the right half.

59. **C) is correct.** The mean is the average: $\frac{14 + 18 + 11 + 28 + 23 + 14}{6} = \frac{108}{6} =$ **18**

60. **B) is correct.** Benjamin's bar graph indicates that ten students prefer vanilla, six students prefer strawberry, and twenty-three students prefer chocolate ice cream.

1. **C) is correct.** Reduce coefficients, subtract exponents.

$$\frac{4x^6y^2}{3x^2y^4}$$

$$= \frac{4x^4}{3y^2}$$

2. **B) is correct.** Multiply by the least common denominator to clear the fractions.

$$(12)\frac{x}{3} + (12)\frac{7}{6} = (12)\frac{5}{2}$$

$$4x + 14 = 30$$

$$4x = 16$$

$$x = \mathbf{4}$$

3. **D) is correct.**

$$\text{whole} = \frac{\text{part}}{\text{percent}}$$

$$\frac{96}{0.20} = \mathbf{480}$$

4. **A) is correct.**

$$6x - 7 = 5(2x + 1)$$

$$6x - 7 = 10x + 5$$

$$6x = 10x + 12$$

$$-4x = 12$$

$$x = \mathbf{-3}$$

5. **D) is correct.**

$$\frac{2}{175} = \frac{5}{x}$$

$$2x = 875$$

$$x = \mathbf{437.5}$$

6. **B) is correct.**

$$2 \div 3 = 0.\overline{6} \approx 0.67$$

7. **C) is correct.**

$$3 \times 6\frac{2}{5} = \frac{3}{1} \times \frac{32}{5} = \frac{96}{5} = 19\frac{1}{5}$$

$$100 - 19\frac{1}{5} = \frac{500}{5} - \frac{96}{5} = \frac{404}{5} = 80\frac{4}{5}$$

8. **A) is correct.**

$$0.308 + 0.486 = \mathbf{0.794}$$

9. **D) is correct.**

$$15 \div 3 \times 5 - 10$$

$$= 5 \times 5 - 10$$

$$= 25 - 10$$

$$= \mathbf{15}$$

10. **B) is correct.** At 2400 hours, the 24-hour clock restarts at 0, so adding 3 hours to 2300 would be **0200** hours.

11. **A) is correct.**

$$6.5 \text{ ft} \times \frac{0.3048 \text{ m}}{1 \text{ ft}} = \textbf{1.98 m}$$

12. **B) is correct.** Distribute by multiplying coefficients and adding exponents.

$$3xy(x^2 - 11xy + 10y^2)$$
$$= \textbf{3x}^3\textbf{y} - \textbf{33x}^2\textbf{y}^2 + \textbf{30xy}^3$$

13. **A) is correct.**

$$\text{whole} = \frac{\text{part}}{\text{percent}}$$
$$\frac{135}{0.45} = \textbf{300}$$

14. **A) is correct.** Reduce coefficients, subtract exponents.

$$\frac{10x^9y^6}{5x^3y^2} = \textbf{2x}^6\textbf{y}^4$$

15. **C) is correct.** Multiply by the least common denominator to clear the fractions.

$$(12)\frac{x}{4} + (12)\frac{2}{3} = (12)\frac{29}{12}$$
$$3x + 8 = 29$$
$$3x = 21$$
$$x = \textbf{7}$$

16. **C) is correct.**

$$\frac{1.50}{100} = \frac{x}{85{,}000}$$
$$100x = 127{,}500$$
$$x = \textbf{1275}$$

17. **D) is correct.**

$$\frac{10}{21} \times \frac{14}{25} = \frac{2}{3} \times \frac{2}{5} = \frac{\textbf{4}}{\textbf{15}}$$

18. **B) is correct.**

$$8.653 + 2 + 1.06 = \textbf{11.713}$$

19. **A) is correct.**

11:15 a.m. is 1115 hours.
$$1115 + 400 = \textbf{1515}$$

20. **B) is correct.**

$$\frac{0.029 \text{ mi}}{\text{hr}} \times \frac{5280 \text{ ft}}{\text{mi}} \times \frac{12 \text{ in}}{\text{ft}} \times \frac{1 \text{ hr}}{3600 \text{ sec}} \approx \textbf{0.51 in/sec}$$

21. **D) is correct.**

$$4x - 3(y - 2x)$$
$$= 4x - 3y + 6x$$
$$= 4x + 6x - 3y$$
$$= \textbf{10x} - \textbf{3y}$$

22. **B) is correct.**

$$\text{percent} = \frac{\text{part}}{\text{whole}}$$

$$\frac{800}{2500} = 0.32 = \textbf{32\%}$$

23. **C) is correct.** Reduce coefficients, subtract exponents.

$$\frac{9\,a^7 b^3}{18\,a^2 b^5} = \frac{\boldsymbol{a^5}}{\boldsymbol{2b^2}}$$

24. **A) is correct.**

$$\frac{25}{100} = \frac{12}{x}$$

$$25x = 1200$$

$$x = \textbf{48}$$

25. **C) is correct.**

$$3 \times 1\frac{3}{4} = \frac{3}{1} \times \frac{7}{4} = \frac{21}{4} = \boldsymbol{5\frac{1}{4}}$$

26. **D) is correct.** Multiply coefficients, add exponents.

$$6a^3 b^2 (5a^2 b^5 c) = \boldsymbol{30a^5 b^7 c}$$

27. **A) is correct.**

$$24\frac{1}{2} \div 3\frac{1}{2} = \frac{49}{2} \div \frac{7}{2} = \frac{49}{2} \times \frac{2}{7} = \frac{49}{7} = \textbf{7}$$

28. **B) is correct.**

part = whole × percent

$$81 \times 0.09 = \textbf{7.29}$$

29. **C) is correct.**

$$\frac{12}{100} = \frac{x}{1500}$$

$$100x = 18{,}000$$

$$x = \textbf{180}$$

30. **C) is correct.**

$$65 - 14.46 + 5.8 = \textbf{56.34}$$

31. **D) is correct.** Five and a half hours after 1:00 p.m. is 6:30 p.m., which is **1830**.

32. **B) is correct.**

$$\$285.48 \div 6 = \textbf{\$47.58}$$

33. **D) is correct.**

$$215 \text{ mi} \times \frac{1.61 \text{ km}}{1 \text{ mi}} \approx \textbf{346 km}$$

34. **A) is correct.**

$$2(3x + 4y) + 7(2x - 2y)$$

$$6x + 8y + 14x - 14y$$

$$6x + 14x + 8y - 14y$$

$$\boldsymbol{20x - 6y}$$

35. **C) is correct.**

$$22\frac{1}{2} \times \frac{1}{3} = \frac{45}{2} \times \frac{1}{3} = \frac{15}{2} = \mathbf{7\frac{1}{2}}$$

36. **A) is correct.**

part = whole × percent

$62 \times 0.90 = \mathbf{55.8}$

37. **B) is correct.**

$$\frac{3.5}{2.6} = \frac{10.5}{x}$$

$3.5x = 27.3$

$x = \mathbf{7.8}$

38. **A) is correct.**

$$5\frac{2}{3} \div \frac{1}{3} = \frac{17}{3} \times \frac{3}{1} = \frac{17}{3} \times \frac{3}{1} = \mathbf{17}$$

39. **D) is correct.**

$2.7 \times \$5.40 = \mathbf{\$14.58}$

40. **B) is correct.**

$$\text{whole} = \frac{\text{part}}{\text{percent}}$$

$$\frac{140}{0.35} = \mathbf{400}$$

41. **D) is correct.**

$$\frac{2}{19} = \frac{x}{2014}$$

$19x = 4028$

$x = \mathbf{212}$

42. **A) is correct.**

$$7\frac{1}{3} \div \frac{4}{5} = \frac{22}{3} \div \frac{4}{5} = \frac{22}{3} \times \frac{5}{4} = \frac{11}{3} \times \frac{5}{2} = \frac{55}{6} = \mathbf{9\frac{1}{6}}$$

43. **C) is correct.**

$6.2 \times 8.5 = \mathbf{52.7}$

44. **B) is correct.**

$$\text{percent} = \frac{\text{part}}{\text{whole}}$$

$$\frac{88}{160} = 0.55 = \mathbf{55\%}$$

45. **D) is correct.**

$\$3.49 \times 6 = \$20.94$

$\$10.49 \times 3 = \$31.47$

$\$20.94 + \$31.47 = \$52.41$

$\$100.00 - \$52.41 = \mathbf{\$47.59}$

46. **B) is correct.**

$$8 \div \frac{2}{3} = \frac{8}{1} \times \frac{3}{2} = \frac{4}{1} \times \frac{3}{1} = \mathbf{12}$$

47.   B) is correct.
$24.96 ÷ 2.4 = **$10.40**

48.   C) is correct.
$11.50 - 9.75 = 1.75$
$percent = \dfrac{part}{whole}$
$\dfrac{1.75}{9.75} \approx 0.179 = \textbf{17.9\%}$

49.   C) is correct.
$8 \div 1\dfrac{1}{3} = \dfrac{8}{1} \div \dfrac{4}{3} = \dfrac{8}{1} \times \dfrac{3}{4} = \textbf{6}$

50.   C) is correct.
$14 \div 52 \approx \textbf{0.269}$

FOUR: SCIENCE

The Biological Hierarchy

The biological hierarchy is a systematic breakdown of the structures of the human body organized from smallest to largest (or largest to smallest). The human body is made up of small units called cells. A cell is a microscopic, self-replicating, structural, and functional unit of the body that performs many different jobs. The cell is made up of many smaller units that are sometimes considered to be part of the biological hierarchy.

- The **mitochondria** are the organelles responsible for making ATP within the cell. Mitochondria have several layers of membranes used to assist the electron transport chain. This pathway uses energy provided by molecules such as glucose or fat (lipid) to generate ATP through the transfer of electrons.

- A **vacuole** is a small body used to transfer materials within and out of the cell. It has a membrane of its own and can carry things such as cell wastes, sugars, or proteins.

- The **nucleus** of a eukaryotic cell contains all of its genetic information in the form of DNA. In the nucleus, DNA replication and transcription occur. In the eukaryotic cell, after transcription, the mRNA is exported out of the nucleus into the cytosol for use.

- The **endoplasmic reticulum (ER)** is used for translation of mRNA into proteins and for the transport of proteins out of the cell. The rough endoplasmic reticulum has many ribosomes attached to it, which function as the cell's machinery in transforming RNA into protein. The smooth endoplasmic reticulum is associated with the production of fats and steroid hormones.

- A **ribosome** is a small two-protein unit that reads mRNA and, with the assistance of transport proteins, creates an amino acid.

- The **Golgi apparatus** collects, packages, and distributes the proteins produced by ribosomes.

- **Chloroplasts** are plant organelles where the reactions of photosynthesis take place.

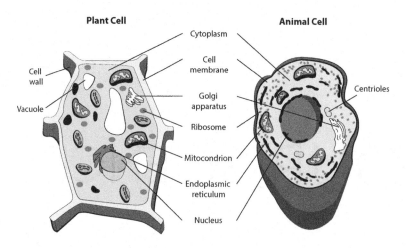

Figure 4.1. Plant and Animal Cell Organelles

Tissues compose the next-largest group of structures in the body. They are a collection of cells that all perform a similar function. The human body has four basic types of tissue:

- **Connective tissues**—which include bones, ligaments, and cartilage—support, separate, or connect the body's various organs and tissues.

- **Epithelial tissues** are thin layers of cells that line blood vessels, body cavities, and some organs.

- **Muscular tissues** contain contractile units that pull on connective tissues to create movement.

- **Nervous tissues** make up the peripheral nervous systems that transmit impulses throughout the body.

After tissues, **organs** are the next-largest structure in the biological hierarchy. Organs are a collection of tissues within the body that share a similar function. For example, the esophagus is an organ whose primary function is carrying food and liquids from the mouth to the stomach.

Organ systems, a group of organs that work together to perform a similar function, rank above organs as the next-largest structure on the biological hierarchy. The esophagus is part of the digestive organ system, which is the entire group of organs in the body that processes food from start to finish.

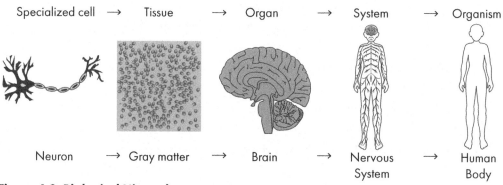

Figure 4.2. Biological Hierarchy

Finally, an **organism** is the total collection of all the parts of the biological hierarchy working together to form a living being; it is the largest structure in the biological hierarchy.

PRACTICE QUESTIONS

1. The meninges are membranes that surround and protect the brain and spinal cord. What type of tissue would the meninges be classified as?

    A) connective tissues

    B) epithelial tissues

    C) muscular tissues

    D) nervous tissues

2. Muscle tissues will often require quick bursts of energy. As a result, which of the following organelles would be most likely to be found in higher than normal amounts in muscle cells?

    A) ribosomes

    B) chloroplasts

    C) vacuoles

    D) mitochondria

DIRECTIONAL TERMINOLOGY

When discussing anatomy and physiology, specific terms are used to refer to directions.

Table 4.1. Anatomical Directions

Term	Meaning	Example
inferior	away from the head	The pelvis is inferior to the head.
superior	closer to the head	The head is superior to the pelvis.
anterior	toward the front	The eyes are anterior to the ears.
posterior	toward the back	The ears are posterior to the eyes.
ventral	toward the front	The stomach is ventral to the spine.
dorsal	toward the back	The spine is dorsal to the stomach.
medial	toward the midline of the body	The heart is medial to the arm.
lateral	further from the midline of the body	The arm is lateral to the chest.
proximal	closer to the trunk	The knee is proximal to the ankle.
distal	away from the trunk	The ankle is distal to the knee.

CHECK YOUR UNDERSTANDING

How would you use anatomical terms to describe the relative positions of the heart and lungs?

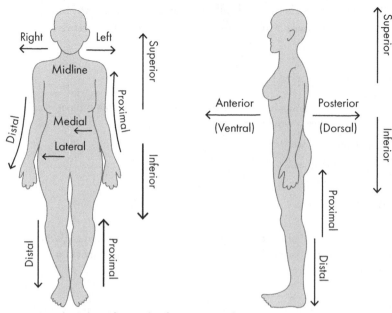

Figure 4.3. Directional Terminology

PRACTICE QUESTION

3. Where is the wrist located relative to the elbow?
    A) distal
    B) proximal
    C) anterior
    D) posterior

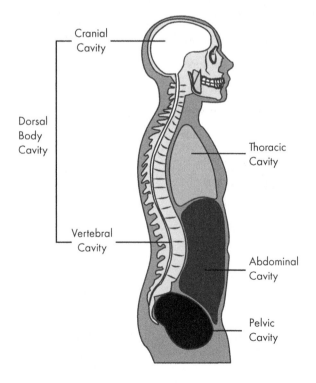

Figure 4.3. Body Cavities

BODY CAVITIES AND PLANES

The internal structure of the human body is organized into compartments called **cavities**, which are separated by membranes. There are two main cavities in the human body: the **dorsal cavity** and the **ventral cavity** (both named for their relative positions).

The dorsal cavity is further divided into the **cranial cavity**, which holds the brain, and the **spinal cavity**, which surrounds the spine. The two sections of the dorsal cavity are continuous. Both sections are lined by the **meninges**, a three-layered membrane that protects the brain and spinal cord.

The ventral cavity houses most of the body's organs. It can be further divided into smaller cavities. The **thoracic cavity** holds the heart and lungs, the **abdominal cavity** holds the digestive organs and kidneys, and the **pelvic cavity** holds the bladder and reproductive organs. Both the abdominal and pelvic cavities are enclosed by a membrane called the **peritoneum**.

The human body is divided by three imaginary planes.

- The **transverse plane** divides the body into a top and bottom half.

- The **frontal** (or coronal) **plane** divides the body into a front and back half.

- The **sagittal plane** divides the body into a right and left half.

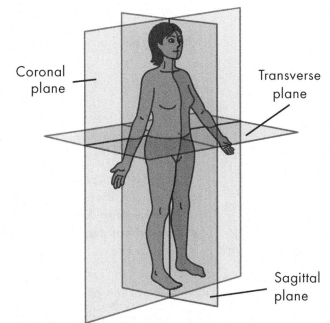

Figure 4.5. Planes of the Human Body

PRACTICE QUESTION

4.   Which body cavity holds the appendix?
    A) dorsal
    B) thoracic
    C) abdominal
    D) pelvic

The Cardiovascular System

STRUCTURE OF BLOOD

The cardiovascular system circulates **blood**, which carries nutrients, waste products, hormones, and other important substances throughout the body. **Plasma** (also called blood plasma) is the liquid part of the blood. Elements suspended or dissolved in the plasma include gases, electrolytes, carbohydrates, fats, proteins, clotting factors, and waste products.

Red blood cells (RBCs) transport oxygen throughout the body. RBCs contain **hemoglobin**, a large molecule with iron atoms that bind to oxygen. **White blood cells (WBCs)** fight infection. **Platelets** (also called thrombocytes) gather at sites of damage in blood vessels as part of the blood-clotting process.

Blood groups (also called blood types) are determined by the presence of **antigens**, proteins that activate antibodies. Each blood group produces specific antibodies that attach to antigens on RBCs. The **ABO blood group** is defined by the presence or absence of A antigens and B antigens.

DID YOU KNOW?
Thrombocytopenia is an abnormally low level of platelets.

Table 4.2. The ABO Blood Groups

Blood Type	Antigens on RBC	Antibodies in Plasma
A	A antigens	anti-B antibodies
B	B antigens	anti-A antibodies
O	no antigens	anti-A and anti-B antibodies
AB	A and B antigens	no antibodies

DID YOU KNOW?

Pregnant patients who are Rh-negative receive a shot that prevents their body from producing anti-Rh antibodies. This protects the fetus from hemolytic disease.

The Rh blood group is defined by the presence of **Rh factor**, an antigen also called the D antigen. The blood type **Rh-positive** has Rh factor antigens on RBCs; the blood type **Rh-negative** does not have Rh factor antigens on RBCs. In **hemolytic disease of the newborn**, anti-Rh antibodies in an Rh-negative mother attack the RBCs of her Rh-positive fetus.

THE COAGULATION PROCESS

Hemostasis is the process of stopping blood loss from a damaged blood vessel. Blood loss is stopped through **coagulation**, the process of turning liquid blood into a semisolid clot composed of platelets and red blood cells held together by the protein **fibrin**.

DID YOU KNOW?

Most clotting factors are designated by roman numerals. These numerals give the order in which factors were discovered, not the order in which they are activated.

The process of coagulation is a complex cascade of reactions involving proteins called clotting factors.

- Platelet aggregation is initiated by the exposure to von **Willebrand factor (vW)** and **tissue factor (TF)**.

- During coagulation, the protein **fibrinogen** (factor I) is converted to fibrin by the enzyme **thrombin** (factor IIa).

- **Prothrombin** (factor II) is a precursor to thrombin.

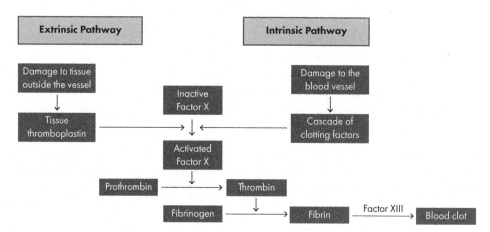

Figure 4.6. Clotting Cascade

STRUCTURE AND FUNCTION OF THE CARDIOVASCULAR SYSTEM

Blood is circulated by a muscular organ called the **heart**. The human heart has four chambers, the right and left **atria** and the right and left **ventricles**, as shown in

Figure 4.7. Each chamber is isolated by valves that prevent the backflow of blood once it has passed through. The **tricuspid** and **mitral valves** separate atria from ventricles, and the **pulmonary** and **aortic valves** regulate the movement of blood out of the heart into the arteries. The pumping action of the heart is regulated primarily by two neurological **nodes**, the **sinoatrial** and the **atrioventricular** nodes, whose electrical activity sets the rhythm of the heart.

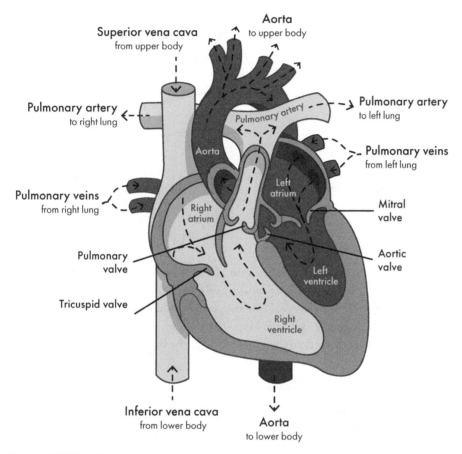

Figure 4.7. The Heart

The heart includes several layers of tissue:

- **pericardium:** the outermost protective layer of the heart that contains a lubricative liquid

- **epicardium:** the deepest layer of the pericardium that envelops the heart muscle

- **myocardium:** the heart muscle

- **endocardium:** the innermost, smooth layer of the heart walls

Blood leaves the heart and travels throughout the body in blood vessels, which decrease in diameter as they move away from the heart and toward the tissues and organs. Blood exits the heart through **arteries**, which become **arterioles** and then **capillaries**, the smallest branch of the circulatory system in which gas exchange from blood to tissues occurs. Deoxygenated blood travels back to the heart through **veins**.

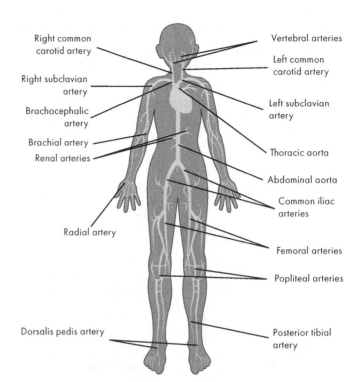

DID YOU KNOW?

The **pulmonary veins** carry blood from the lungs to the heart and are the only veins in the human body that carry oxygenated blood.

Figure 4.8. Major Arteries

The circulatory system includes two closed loops. In the **pulmonary loop**, deoxygenated blood leaves the heart and travels to the lungs, where it loses carbon dioxide and becomes rich in oxygen. The oxygenated blood then returns to the heart, which pumps it through the systemic loop. The **systemic loop** delivers oxygen to the rest of the body and returns deoxygenated blood to the heart.

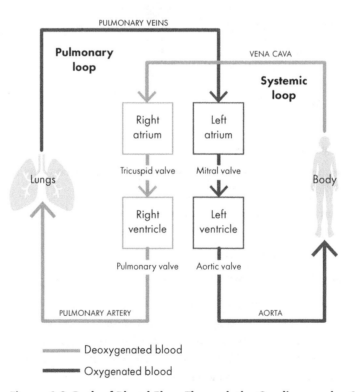

Figure 4.9. Path of Blood Flow Through the Cardiovascular System

THE LYMPHATIC SYSTEM

The **lymphatic system** operates alongside the circulatory system to move fluids and other substances through a system of **lymphatic vessels**. It is particularly important for immune system functioning because it circulates white blood cells. It also removes waste products and balances fluid levels by removing excess interstitial fluid (the fluid between cells).

Lymph, the fluid carried through the lymphatic system, passes through lymph nodes. These nodes filter waste from the lymph and are also home to large numbers of white blood cells. After it has been filtered, lymph is returned to the cardiovascular system through the subclavian vein.

PATHOLOGIES OF THE CARDIOVASCULAR SYSTEM

Hypertension is increased blood pressure, usually above 140/80 mm Hg. Hypertension usually has no symptoms, but it has been linked to heart disease and stroke. **Hypotension** is decreased blood pressure, usually below 90/60 mm Hg.

Ischemia is reduced or restricted blood flow to tissues, and **infarction** is the death of tissue caused by restricted blood flow and the subsequent lack of oxygen. Causes of ischemia include:

- occlusion of blood vessels by an **embolus** (a mass made of fat, bacteria, or other materials) or a **thrombus** (blood clot; also called a thromboembolism)
- narrowed blood vessel (e.g., aneurysm or atherosclerosis)
- trauma

A **myocardial infarction** (MI; also called a heart attack) is an occlusion of the coronary arteries, which supply blood to the heart. The resulting death of cardiac tissue may lead to dysrhythmias, reduced cardiac output, or cardiac arrest. Patients with MI require immediate medical intervention to restore blood flow to the coronary arteries.

Atherosclerosis is a progressive condition in which **plaque** (composed of fat, white blood cells, and other waste) builds up in the arteries. The presence of advanced atherosclerosis places patients at a high risk for several cardiovascular conditions, including blocked or narrowed blood vessels.

- **Dysrhythmias** are abnormal heart rhythms.
- **Bradycardia** is a heart rate < 60 bpm, and **tachycardia** is a heart rate > 100 bpm.
- **Ventricular fibrillation** (**V-fib**) and **ventricular tachycardia** (**V-tach**) are dangerous types of tachycardia that can be corrected with shocks from an automatic external defibrillator (AED).
- **Asystole**, also called a "flat line," occurs when there is no electrical or mechanical activity within the heart. It is a non-shockable rhythm with a poor survival rate.

Heart failure occurs when either one or both of the ventricles in the heart cannot efficiently pump blood. Because the heart is unable to pump effectively, blood and fluid back up into the lungs (causing pulmonary congestion), or the fluid builds up

HELPFUL HINT

Common symptoms of MI include pain or pressure in the chest, jaw, or arm; sweating; nausea/vomiting; and pallor. Some patients, especially women or people with diabetes, may present without chest pain.

peripherally (causing edema of the lower extremities). Heart failure is most commonly categorized into left-sided heart failure or right-sided heart failure, although both sides of the heart can fail at the same time.

Hemophilia is a recessive X-chromosome–linked bleeding disorder characterized by the lack of coagulation factors. **Sickle cell disease** is an inherited form of hemolytic anemia that causes deformities in the shape of the RBCs.

PRACTICE QUESTIONS

5. What function do red blood cells perform in the human body?
   A) fight infection
   B) transport oxygen
   A) hydrate cells
   B) carry nutrients

6. Von Willebrand disease is caused by low levels or poor quality of von Willebrand factor. What signs and symptoms would a patient with von Willebrand disease likely have?
   A) nosebleeds
   B) rapid heartbeat
   C) trouble breathing
   D) headache

7. Which of the following layers of the wall of the heart contains cardiac muscles?
   A) myocardium
   B) epicardium
   C) endocardium
   D) pericardium

8. The blood from the right ventricle goes to
   A) the left atria.
   B) the vena cava.
   C) the aorta.
   D) the lungs.

9. The blood vessels that carry the blood from the heart are called
   A) veins.
   B) venules.
   C) capillaries.
   D) arteries.

The Respiratory System
STRUCTURE AND FUNCTION OF THE RESPIRATORY SYSTEM

The **respiratory system** is responsible for the exchange of gases between the human body and the environment. **Oxygen** is brought into the body for use in glucose metabolism, and the **carbon dioxide** created by glucose metabolism is expelled. Gas exchange takes place in the **lungs**. Humans have two lungs, a right and a left, and the right lung is slightly larger than the left. The right lung has three **lobes**, and the left has two. The lungs are surrounded by a thick membrane called the **pleura**.

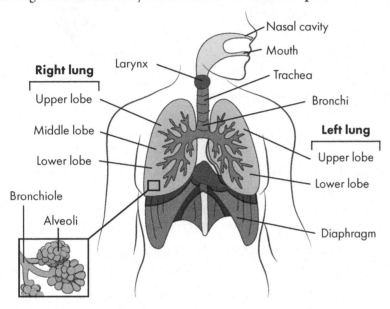

Figure 4.10. The Respiratory System

Respiration begins with **pulmonary ventilation**, or breathing. The first stage of breathing is **inhalation**. During this process, the thoracic cavity expands and the diaphragm muscle contracts, which decreases the pressure in the lungs, pulling in air from the atmosphere. Air is drawn in through the nose and mouth, then into the throat, where cilia and mucus filter out particles before the air enters the **trachea**. During inspiration, the **epiglottis** covers the esophagus so that air does not enter the digestive track.

Once it passes through the trachea, the air passes through either the left or right **bronchi**, which are divisions of the trachea that direct air into the left or right lung. These bronchi are further divided into smaller **bronchioles**, which branch throughout the lungs and become increasingly small.

Eventually, air enters the **alveoli**—tiny air sacs located at the ends of the smallest bronchioles. The alveoli have very thin membranes, only one cell thick, and are the location of gas exchange with the blood: oxygen diffuses into the blood while carbon dioxide is diffused out.

Carbon dioxide is then expelled from the lungs during **exhalation**, the second stage of breathing. During exhalation, the diaphragm relaxes and the thoracic cavity contracts, causing air to leave the body, as the lung pressure is now greater than the atmospheric pressure.

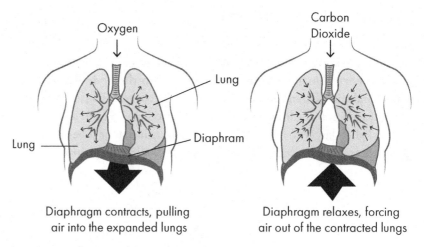

Oxygen

Lung

Lung

Diaphram

Diaphragm contracts, pulling
air into the expanded lungs

Carbon
Dioxide

Diaphragm relaxes, forcing
air out of the contracted lungs

Figure 4.11. The Breathing Process

PATHOLOGIES OF THE RESPIRATORY SYSTEM

Lung diseases that result in the continual restriction of airflow are known as **chronic obstructive pulmonary disease (COPD)**. These include **emphysema**, which is the destruction of lung tissues, and **asthma**, in which the airways are compromised due to a dysfunctional immune response. The main causes of COPD are smoking and air pollution, and genetic factors can also influence the severity of the disease.

A **pulmonary embolism** is a blood clot (usually originating in the legs) that travels to the lungs, causing chest pain, shortness of breath, and low blood oxygen levels.

The respiratory system is also prone to **respiratory tract infections**, with upper respiratory tract infections affecting air inputs in the nose and throat, and lower respiratory tract infections affecting the lungs and their immediate pulmonary inputs. Viral infections of the respiratory system include **influenza** and the **common cold**; bacterial infections include **tuberculosis** and **pertussis** (whooping cough). **Pneumonia**, the inflammation of the lungs that affects alveoli, can be caused by bacteria, viruses, fungi, or parasites. It is often seen in people whose respiratory system has been weakened by other conditions.

Lung cancer is the second-most common type of cancer diagnosed in the United States. (Breast cancer is the most common.) Symptoms of lung cancer include cough, chest pain, and wheezing. Lung cancer is most often caused by smoking, but it can develop in nonsmokers as well.

PRACTICE QUESTIONS

10. During respiration, the epiglottis prevents air from entering which of the following organs?

A) bronchi

B) pharynx

C) larynx

D) esophagus

11. Which of the following structures are small air sacs that function as the site of gas exchange in the lungs?

    A) capillaries

    B) bronchi

    C) alveoli

    D) cilia

12. Which of the following conditions is caused by an immune response?

    A) COPD

    B) influenza

    C) asthma

    D) emphysema

The Nervous System

STRUCTURE AND FUNCTION OF THE NERVOUS SYSTEM

The **nervous system** coordinates the processes and actions of the human body. **Nerve cells**, or **neurons**, communicate through electrical impulses and allow the body to process and respond to stimuli. Neurons have a nucleus and transmit electrical impulses through their axons and dendrites. The **axon** is the stemlike structure, often covered in a fatty insulating substance called **myelin**, that carries information to other neurons throughout the body. Myelin is produced by **Schwann cells**, which also play an important role in nerve regeneration. **Dendrites** receive information from other neurons.

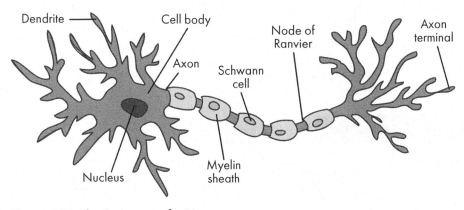

Figure 4.12. The Structure of a Neuron

The nervous system is broken down into two parts: the **central nervous system (CNS)** and the **peripheral nervous system (PNS)**. The CNS is made up of the brain and spinal cord. The brain acts as the control center for the body and is responsible for nearly all the body's processes and actions. The spinal cord relays information between the brain and the peripheral nervous system; it also coordinates many reflexes. The spinal cord is protected by the vertebral column, a structure of bones that enclose the delicate nervous tissue. The PNS is the collection of nerves that connect the central nervous system to the rest of the body.

The functions of the nervous system are broken down into the autonomic nervous system and the somatic nervous system. The **autonomic nervous system** controls involuntary actions that occur in the body, such as respiration, heartbeat, digestive processes, and more. The **somatic nervous system** is responsible for the body's ability to control skeletal muscles and voluntary movement as well as the involuntary reflexes associated with skeletal muscles.

The autonomic nervous system is further broken down into the sympathetic nervous system and the parasympathetic nervous system. The **sympathetic nervous system** is responsible for the body's reaction to stress and induces a "fight-or-flight" response to stimuli. For instance, if an individual is frightened, the sympathetic nervous system increases in the person's heart rate and blood pressure to prepare them to either fight or flee

In contrast, the **parasympathetic nervous system** is stimulated by the body's need for rest or recovery. The parasympathetic nervous system responds by decreasing heart rate, blood pressure, and muscular activation when a person is getting ready for activities such as sleeping or digesting food. For example, the body activates the parasympathetic nervous system after eating a large meal, which is why people then feel sluggish.

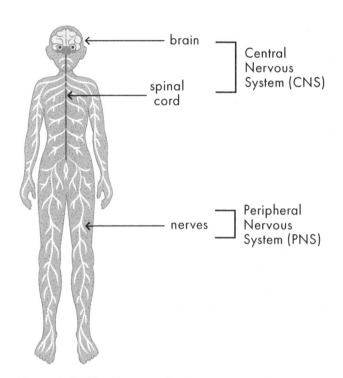

Figure 4.13. The Nervous System

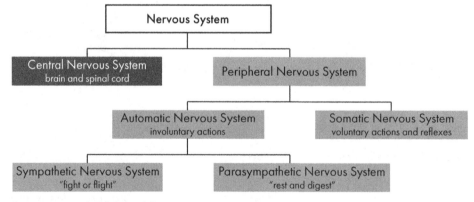

Figure 4.14. Divisions of the Nervous System

DID YOU KNOW?
The fight-or-flight reaction includes accelerated breathing and heart rate, dilation of blood vessels in muscles, release of energy molecules for use by muscles, relaxation of the bladder, and slowed or stopped movement in the upper digestive tract.

SENSORY SYSTEM

The **sensory nervous system** processes sensory information. The process of sensing starts with **sensory neurons**, which receive signals from the environment or body. There are five main types of sensory neurons:

- **Chemoreceptors** detect chemical stimuli.

- **Photoreceptors** detect light.

- **Mechanoreceptors** detect pressure, vibration, and texture.
- **Thermoreceptors** detect temperature.
- **Nociceptors** detect pain.

Signals from sensory neurons travel along neurons to the brain, where specialized areas process the signals. For example, sensory neurons in the ear pass signals along the auditory nerve to the primary auditory cortex. Similarly, sensory information from photoreceptors in the eye travel along the optic nerve to the visual cortex.

There are five "traditional senses": vision, taste, smell, taste, and touch. Other senses include nociception (pain), proprioception (sense of body position), and equilibrioception (sense of balance).

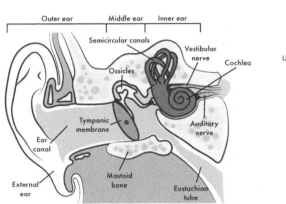

Figure 4.15. Anatomy of the Ear

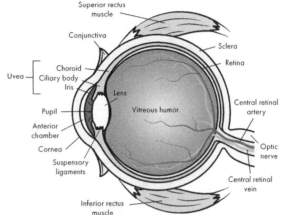

Figure 4.16. Anatomy of the Eye

PATHOLOGIES OF THE NERVOUS SYSTEM

A **stroke**, or **cardiovascular accident (CVA)**, occurs when blood flow to brain tissue is disrupted. An **ischemic stroke** is the result of a blockage (embolus) in the vasculature of the brain. A **hemorrhagic stroke** is bleeding in the brain, often caused by a ruptured aneurysm.

The nervous system can be affected by a number of degenerative diseases that result from the gradual breakdown of nervous tissue. These include:

- **Parkinson's disease**: caused by cell death in the basal ganglia; characterized by gradual loss of motor function
- **multiple sclerosis (MS)**: caused by damage to the myelin sheath; characterized by muscle spasms and weakness, numbness, loss of coordination, and blindness
- **amyotrophic lateral sclerosis (ALS)**: caused by the death of neurons that control voluntary muscle movement; characterized by muscle stiffness, twitches, and weakness
- **Alzheimer's disease**: caused by damaged neurons in the cerebral cortex; characterized by memory loss, confusion, mood swings, and problems with language

The nervous system is also susceptible to infections, some of which can be life threatening. **Meningitis** is inflammation of the meninges, the protective membrane that surrounds the brain and spinal cord, and **encephalitis** is inflammation of the brain. Both conditions can be caused by viral or bacterial pathogens.

Epileptic seizures are brief episodes caused by disturbed or overactive nerve cell activity in the brain. Seizures range widely in severity and may include confusion, convulsions, and loss of consciousness. They have many causes, including tumors, infections, head injuries, and medications.

PRACTICE QUESTIONS

13. Which of the following parts of a neuron is responsible for carrying information away from the cell?

    A) soma

    B) axon

    C) dendrite

    D) myelin

14. Which part of the nervous system controls only voluntary action?

    A) the peripheral nervous system

    B) the somatic nervous system

    C) the sympathetic nervous system

    D) the parasympathetic nervous system

15. What substance does a Schwann cell secrete that increases the speed of signals traveling to and from neurons?

    A) myelin

    B) cerebrospinal fluid

    C) corpus callosum

    D) collagen

The Skeletal System
STRUCTURE AND FUNCTION OF THE SKELETAL SYSTEM

The skeletal system is made up of over 200 different **bones**, a stiff connective tissue in the human body with many functions, including:

- protecting internal organs

- synthesizing blood cells

- storing necessary minerals, particularly calcium

- providing the muscular system with leverage to create movement

Bones are covered with a thin layer of vascular connective tissue called the **periosteum**, which serves as a point of muscle attachment, supplies blood to the bone, and contains nerve endings. **Osseous tissue** is the primary tissue that makes up bone. There are two types of osseous tissue: cortical (compact) bone and cancellous (spongy)

HELPFUL HINT

Osteoclasts are a type of bone cell responsible for breaking down bone tissue. They are located on the surface of bones and help balance the body's calcium levels by degrading bone to release stored calcium.

bone. **Cortical bone** is the dense, solid material that surrounds the bone and gives it hardness and strength. It is usually concentrated in the middle part of the bone.

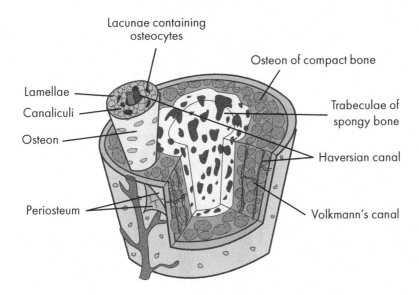

Figure 4.17. Structure of Bone

Cancellous bone is less dense, more porous, and softer. It is located at the ends of long bones, where it does not bear a structural load. Instead, it is a site of the bone's blood production and metabolic activity, as it stores both blood vessels and **bone marrow**. **Red bone marrow** houses **stem cells**, which are made into red blood cells, platelets, and white blood cells (a process called hematopoiesis). **Yellow bone marrow** is composed mostly of fat tissue and can be converted to red bone marrow in response to extreme blood loss in the body.

Table 4.3. Types of Bones

Name	Shape	Example
Long bones	longer than they are wide	femur, humerus
Short bones	wider than they are long	clavicle, carpals
Flat bones	wide and flat	skull, pelvis
Irregular bones	irregularly shaped	vertebrae, jaw

The hundreds of bones in the body make up the human **skeleton**. The **axial skeleton** contains eighty bones and has three major subdivisions: the **skull**, which contains the cranium and facial bones; the **thorax**, which includes the sternum and twelve pairs of ribs; and the **vertebral column**, which contains the body's thirty-three vertebrae. These eighty bones function together to support and protect many of the body's vital organs, including the brain, lungs, heart, and spinal cord. The **appendicular skeleton**'s 126 bones make up the body's appendages. The main function of the appendicular skeleton is locomotion.

CHECK YOUR UNDERSTANDING

How might diet affect the body's ability to rebuild bone after a fracture?

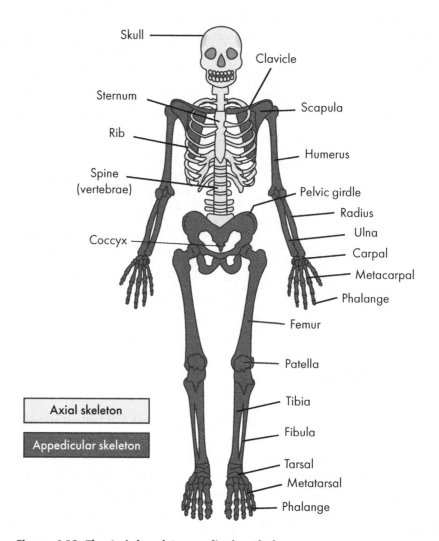

Figure 4.18. The Axial and Appendicular Skeletons

Various connective tissues join the parts of the skeleton to other systems, as shown in the table below.

Table 4.4. Connective Tissue in the Skeletal System

Tissue	Function
Ligament	Joins bone to bone.
Tendon	Joins bones to muscles.
Cartilage	Cushions bones in joints. Provides structural integrity for many body parts (e.g., the ears and nose) and maintains open pathways (e.g., the trachea and bronchi).

JOINTS

The point at which a bone is attached to another bone is called a joint. There are three basic types of joints:

- **Fibrous joints** connect bones that do not move.
- **Cartilaginous joints** connect bones with cartilage and allow limited movement.
- **Synovial joints** allow for a range of motion and are covered by articular cartilage that protects the bones.

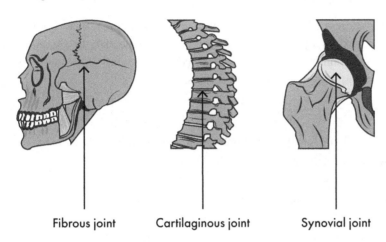

Fibrous joint   Cartilaginous joint   Synovial joint

Figure 4.19. Types of Joints

Synovial joints are classified based on their structure and the type of movement they allow. There are many types of synovial joints; the most important are discussed in Table 4.5.

Table 4.5. Types of Synovial Joints

Name	Movement	Found In
Hinge joint	lmovement through one plane of motion as flexion/extension	elbows, knees, fingers
Ball-and-socket joint	range of motion through multiple planes and rotation about an axis	hips, shoulders
Saddle joint	movement through multiple planes, but cannot rotate about an axis	thumbs
Gliding joint	sliding movement in the plane of the bones' surfaces	vertebrae, small bones in the wrists and ankles
Condyloid joint	movement through two planes as flexion/extension and abduction/adduction, but cannot rotate about an axis	wrists
Pivot joint	only movement is rotation about an axis	elbows, neck

Arthritis is inflammation in joints that leads to swelling, pain, and reduced range of motion. There are many different kinds of arthritis. The most common is **osteoarthritis**, which is caused by the wearing down of cartilage in the joints due to age or injury. **Rheumatoid arthritis** and **psoriatic arthritis** are both types of inflammation at the joint caused by chronic autoimmune disorder, which can lead to excessive joint degradation.

Osteoporosis refers to poor bone mineral density due to the loss or lack of the production of calcium content and bone cells, which leads to bone brittleness. It is most common in postmenopausal women.

Bone cancers include Ewing's sarcoma and osteosarcoma. In addition, white blood cell cancers, such as myeloma and leukemia, start in bone marrow. **Osteomyelitis** is an infection in the bone that can occur directly (after a traumatic bone injury) or indirectly (via the vascular system or other infected tissues).

PRACTICE QUESTIONS

16. Stem cells are found in which of the following tissues?
    A) red bone marrow
    B) cartilage
    C) compact bones
    D) bone matrix

17. Which of the following parts of the skeletal system is formed from long bones?
    A) limbs
    B) thoracic cage
    C) skull
    D) vertebral column

18. Which of the following is released when bone is broken down?
    A) phosphorous
    B) iron
    C) calcium
    D) zinc

The Muscular System

The primary function of the muscular system is movement. Muscles contract and relax, resulting in motion. This includes both voluntary motion, such as walking, as well as involuntary motion that maintains the body's systems, such as circulation, respiration, and digestion. Other functions of the muscular system include overall stability and protection of the spine as well as posture.

MUSCLE CELL STRUCTURE

The main structural unit of a muscle is the **sarcomere**. Sarcomeres are composed of a series of **muscle fibers**, which are elongated individual cells that stretch from one end of the muscle to the other. Within each fiber are hundreds of **myofibrils**, long strands within the cells that contain alternating layers of thin filaments made of the protein **actin** and thick filaments made of the protein **myosin**. Each of these proteins plays a role in muscle contraction and relaxation. During muscle contractions, myosin pulls the thin filaments of actin to the center of the sarcomere, causing the entire sarcomere to shorten, or contract, creating movement.

Skeletal muscles are activated by special neurons called **motor neurons**. Together, a motor neuron and its associated skeletal muscle fibers are called a **motor unit**. These motor neurons are located within the spinal cord and branch out to the muscles to send the nervous impulses for muscular contraction. The **neuromuscular junction** is the site at which the motor neuron and muscle fibers join to form a chemical synapse for nervous transmission to muscle.

TYPES OF MUSCLES

The muscular system consists of three types of muscle: cardiac, visceral, and skeletal. **Cardiac muscle** is only found in the heart and contracts involuntarily, creating the heartbeat and pumping blood. **Visceral muscles** are found in many of the body's essential organs, including the stomach and intestines. They slowly contract and relax to move nutrients, blood, and other substances throughout the body. Visceral muscles are also known as **smooth muscles** because, unlike cardiac and skeletal muscle, this tissue is not composed of sarcomeres with alternating thick and thin filaments. Visceral muscle movement is involuntary.

Skeletal muscle is responsible for voluntary movement and, as the name suggests, is inextricably linked to the skeletal system. Skeletal muscles can engage in several types of muscle actions:

- **concentric**: muscular contraction in which the length of the muscle is shortening to lift the resistance (upward curl of bicep)

- **eccentric**: muscular contraction in which the muscle is resisting a force as it lengthens (downward curl of bicep)

- **isometric**: muscular contraction in which the resistance and force are even and no movement is taking place (holding an object)

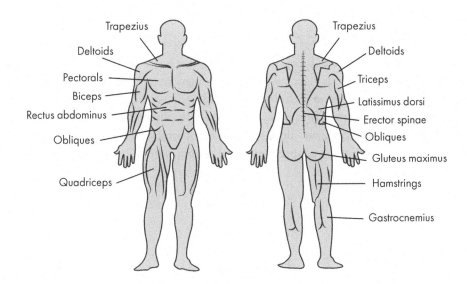

Figure 4.20. Major Muscles of the Body

PATHOLOGIES OF THE MUSCULAR SYSTEM

Injuries to muscle can impede movement and cause pain. When muscle fibers are over-stretched, the resulting **muscle strain** can cause pain, stiffness, and bruising. Muscle **cramps** are involuntary muscle contractions (or **spasms**) that cause intense pain.

Muscle fibers can also be weakened by diseases, as with **muscular dystrophy (MD)**. MD is a genetically inherited condition that results in progressive muscle wasting, which limits movement and can cause respiratory and cardiovascular difficulties.

Rhabdomyolysis is the rapid breakdown of dead muscle tissue. It is usually caused by crush injuries, overexertion (particularly in extreme heat), and a variety of drugs and toxins (particularly statins, which are prescribed to lower cholesterol levels).

PRACTICE QUESTIONS

19. Which of the following types of muscle is found in blood vessels?
    A) cardiac muscle
    B) visceral muscle
    C) type I muscle fibers
    D) type II muscle fibers

20. Which of the following processes is performed by myofibrils?
    A) sugar storage
    B) electrochemical communication
    C) lactic acid fermentation
    D) muscle contractions

21. Which of the following causes a muscle strain?
    A) a lack of available energy
    B) the inability of muscle fibers to contract
    C) detachment of the ligament from the bone
    D) overstretching of muscle fibers

The Immune System

STRUCTURE AND FUNCTION OF THE IMMUNE SYSTEM

The human immune system protects the body against bacteria and viruses that cause disease. The system is composed of two parts, the innate system and the adaptive system. The **innate immune system** includes nonspecific defenses that work against a wide range of infectious agents. This system includes both physical barriers that keep out foreign particles and organisms along with cells that attack invaders. The second part of the immune system is the **adaptive immune system**, which "learns" to respond only to specific invaders.

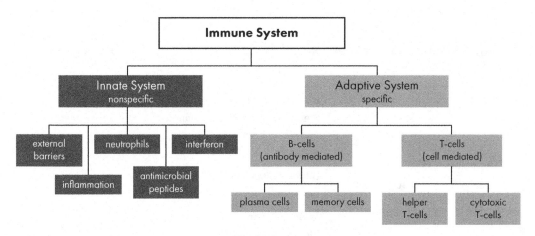

Figure 4.21. Divisions of the Immune System

Barriers to entry are the first line of defense in the immune system:

- The skin leaves few openings for an infection-causing agent to enter.

- Native bacteria outcompete invaders in openings.

- The urethra flushes out invaders with the outflow of urine.

- Mucus and earwax trap pathogens before they can replicate and cause infection.

However, pathogens can breach these barriers and enter the body, where they attempt to replicate and cause an infection. When this occurs, the body mounts a number of nonspecific responses. The body's initial response is **inflammation**, which increases blood flow to the infected area. This increase in blood flow increases the presence of white blood cells, also called **leukocytes**. (The types of white blood cells are discussed in Table 7.4.) Other innate responses include **antimicrobial peptides**, which destroy bacteria by interfering with the functions of their membranes or DNA, and **interferon**, which causes nearby cells to increase their defenses.

The adaptive immune system relies on molecules called **antigens** that appear on the surface of pathogens to which the system has previously been exposed. Antigens are displayed on the surface of cells by the **major histocompatibility complex (MHC)**.

In the cell-mediated response, **T-cells** destroy any cell that displays an antigen. In the antibody-mediated response, **B-cells** are activated by antigens. These B-cells produce plasma cells, which in turn release antibodies. **Antibodies** will bind only to specific antigens and destroy the infected cell. **Memory B-cells** are created during infection, allowing the immune system to respond more quickly if the infection appears again.

HELPFUL HINT

Memory B-cells are the underlying mechanisms behind some vaccines, which introduce a harmless version of a pathogen into the body to activate the body's adaptive immune response.

Table 4.6. Types of White Blood Cells

Type of Cell	Name of Cell	Role	Innate or Adaptive	Prevalence
Granulocytes	neutrophil	first responders that quickly migrate to the site of infections to destroy bacterial invaders	innate	very common
	eosinophil	attack multicellular parasites	innate	rare
	basophil	large cell responsible for inflammatory reactions, including allergies	innate	very rare
Lymphocytes	B-cells	vertebrae, small bones in the wrists and ankles	adaptive	common
	T-cells	respond to antigens by destroying invaders and infected cells	adaptive	
	natural killer cells	destroy virus-infected cells and tumor cells	innate and adaptive	
Monocytes	macrophage	engulf and destroy microbes, foreign substances, and cancer cells	innate and adaptive	rare

PATHOLOGIES OF THE IMMUNE SYSTEM

The immune system of individuals with an **autoimmune disease** will attack healthy tissues. Autoimmune diseases (and the tissues they attack) include:

- psoriasis (skin)
- rheumatoid arthritis (joints)
- multiple sclerosis (nerve cells)
- lupus (kidneys, lungs, and skin)

The immune system may also overreact to harmless particles, a condition known as an **allergy**. Allergic reactions can be mild, resulting in watery eyes and a runny nose, but they can also include life-threatening swelling and respiratory obstruction.

Some infections will attack the immune system itself. **Human immunodeficiency virus (HIV)** attacks helper T-cells, eventually causing **acquired immunodeficiency syndrome (AIDS)**, which allows opportunistic infections to overrun the body. The immune system can also be weakened by previous infections or lifestyle factors such as smoking and alcohol consumption.

Cancers of the immune system include **lymphoma** and **leukemia**, which are caused by irregular growth of cells in lymph and bone marrow. Both white and red blood cells can become cancerous, but it is more common for the cancer to occur in white blood cells. Leukemia is the most common type of cancer to occur in children.

PRACTICE QUESTIONS

22. Which of the following is NOT part of the innate immune system?

    A) interferon

    B) neutrophils

    C) antibodies

    D) natural killer lymphocytes

23. Which of the following is a response by the innate immune system when tissue is damaged?

    A) The skin dries out.

    B) The temperature increases.

    C) The blood flow to the area decreases.

    D) The heart rate slows.

24. What is the role of monocytes in wounds?

    A) They increase blood clotting.

    B) They release histamines.

    C) They digest pathogens.

    D) They prevent inflammation.

The Gastrointestinal System

STRUCTURE AND FUNCTION OF THE GASTROINTESTINAL SYSTEM

The **gastrointestinal system** is responsible for the breakdown and absorption of food necessary to power the body. The gastrointestinal system starts at the **mouth**, which allows for the consumption and mastication of nutrients via an opening in the face. It contains the muscular **tongue** to move food and uses the liquid **saliva** to assist in the breakdown of food.

The chewed and lubricated food travels from the mouth through the **esophagus** via **peristalsis**, the contraction of smooth muscles. The esophagus leads to the **stomach**, the organ of the digestive tract found in the abdominal cavity that mixes food with powerful acidic liquid for further digestion. Once the stomach has created an acidic bolus of digested food known as **chyme**, it travels to the **small intestine**, where a significant amount of nutrient absorption takes place. The tubelike small intestine contains millions of fingerlike projections known as **villi** and microvilli to increase the surface area available for the absorption of nutrients found in food.

The small intestine then transports food to the **large intestine**. The large intestine is similarly tubelike but is larger in diameter than the small intestine. It assists in water absorption, further nutrient absorption, waste collection, and the production of feces for excretion. At the end of the large intestine are the **rectum** and the **anus**, which are responsible for the storage of feces and removal of feces, respectively. The anus is the opening at the opposite end of the digestive tract as the mouth.

HELPFUL HINT

Digestive enzymes work through the GI tract to break down macromolecules to be used in bodily processes.

amylase: breaks down carbohydrates in the mouth

lipase: breaks down lipids in the mouth

pepsin: breaks down proteins in the stomach

lactase: breaks down lactose in the small intestine

protease: breaks down proteins in the small intestine

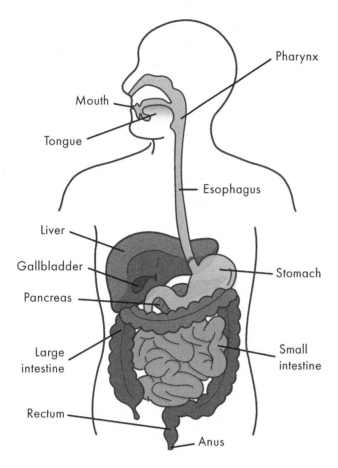

Mouth
Tongue
Pharynx
Esophagus
Liver
Gallbladder
Pancreas
Stomach
Large intestine
Small intestine
Rectum
Anus

Figure 4.22. The Gastrointestinal system

Along the digestive tract are several muscular rings, known as **sphincters**, which regulate the movement of food through the tract and prevent reflux of material into the previous cavity. These include:

- upper esophageal sphincter: between the pharynx and esophagus
- lower esophageal sphincter: between the esophagus and stomach
- pyloric sphincter: between the stomach and small intestine
- ileocecal sphincter: between the small intestine and large intestine
- anus: between the rectum and the outside of the body

The gastrointestinal system also includes accessory organs that aid in digestion:

- **salivary glands**: produce saliva, which begins the process of breaking down starches and fats
- **liver**: produces bile, which helps break down fat in the small intestine
- **gallbladder**: stores bile
- **pancreas**: produces digestive enzymes and pancreatic juice, which neutralizes the acidity of chyme

PATHOLOGIES OF THE GASTROINTESTINAL SYSTEM

The gastrointestinal system is prone to several illnesses of varying severity. Commonly, gastrointestinal distress is caused by an acute infection (bacterial or viral) affecting the lining of the gastrointestinal system that leads to vomiting and diarrhea.

Chronic GI disorders include **irritable bowel syndrome** (the causes of which are largely unknown) and **Crohn's disease**, an inflammatory bowel disorder that occurs when the immune system attacks the gastrointestinal system.

A number of different cancers can arise in the gastrointestinal system, including colon and rectal cancer, liver cancer, pancreatic cancer, esophageal cancer, and stomach cancer. Of these, colon cancer is the most common.

DID YOU KNOW?

The veins of the stomach and intestines do not carry blood directly to the heart. Instead, they divert it to the liver (through the hepatic portal vein) so that the liver can store sugar, remove toxins, and process the products of digestion.

PRACTICE QUESTIONS

25. Which of the following organs does food NOT pass through as part of digestion?

A) stomach

B) large intestine

C) esophagus

D) liver

26. Where in the digestive tract are most of the nutrients absorbed?
    A) the small intestine
    B) the rectum
    C) the stomach
    D) the large intestine

27. What is the role of the liver in digestion?
    A) It produces the bile needed to digest fats.
    B) It stores bile produced by the gallbladder.
    C) It regulates feelings of hunger.
    D) It collects the waste that is the end product of digestion.

The Renal System

STRUCTURE AND FUNCTION OF THE RENAL SYSTEM

The **renal system** excretes water and waste from the body and is crucial for maintaining the balance of water and salt in the blood (also called electrolyte balance). The main organs of the renal system are the **kidneys**, which perform several important functions:

- filter waste from the blood
- maintain the electrolyte balance in the blood
- regulate blood volume, pressure, and pH

The kidneys also function as an endocrine organ and release several important hormones, including **renin**, which regulates blood pressure. The kidney is divided into two regions: the **renal cortex**, which is the outermost layer, and the **renal medulla**, which is the inner layer.

The functional unit of the kidney is the **nephron**, which is a series of looping tubes that filter the blood. The resulting waste includes **urea**, a byproduct of protein catabolism, and **uric acid**, a byproduct of nucleic acid metabolism. Together, these waste products are excreted from the body in **urine**.

Filtration begins in a network of capillaries called a **glomerulus**, which is located in the renal cortex of each kidney. This waste is then funneled into **collecting ducts** in the renal medulla. From the collecting ducts, urine passes through the **renal pelvis** and then through two long tubes called **ureters**. The two ureters drain into the **urinary bladder**, which holds up to 1 liter of liquid. Urine exits the bladder through the **urethra**. In males, the urethra goes through the penis and also carries semen. In females, the much-shorter urethra ends just above the vaginal opening.

ELECTROLYTES

Electrolytes are positively or negatively charged ions located in both the intracellular fluid (ICF) and the extracellular fluid (ECF). These ions are necessary for many bodily function; they are particularly important for cellular communication and membrane transport.

HELPFUL HINT

A **sphincter** is any circular muscle that controls movement of substances through passageways. Sphincters are found throughout the human body, including in the bladder, esophagus, and capillaries.

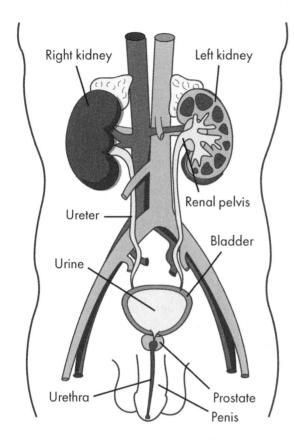

Right kidney

Left kidney

Renal pelvis

Ureter

Bladder

Urine

Urethra

Prostate

Penis

Figure 4.23. The Renal system (Male)

- **Sodium (Na⁺)** is necessary for maintaining ECF volume and for transport across cell membranes. It also maintains cell **membrane potential** (the charge across the cell membrane), which is necessary for nerve cell functioning and muscle contraction.

- **Potassium (K⁺)** works together with sodium to maintain cell membrane potential. It is especially important for muscle functioning, including cardiac muscle.

- **Magnesium (Mg²⁺)** is necessary for ATP metabolism, muscle contraction, and neurological functioning.

- **Calcium (Ca²⁺)** is the main component of bone and also plays a role in nerve cell functioning and muscle contraction.

- **Phosphate (PO₄⁻³)** is a component of many key macromolecules, including ATP and nucleotides.

The balance of electrolytes in the body is primarily maintained by the kidneys, which filter electrolytes from the blood to be excreted in urine. This balance can be upset by environmental conditions or medical disorders. A summary of the symptoms and common causes of electrolyte imbalances is given in the table below.

Table 4.7. Electrolyte Imbalances

Imbalance	Symptoms	Causes
Sodium (normal: 135 – 145 mEq/L)		
Hyponatremia	tachycardia and hypotension weakness and dizziness abdominal cramping increased intracranial pressure seizure	overhydration diarrhea or excessive sweating chronic heart failure
Hypernatremia	tachycardia and hypotension thirst edema and warm, flushed skin hyperreflexia seizure	dehydration renal or GI dysfunction
Potassium (normal: 3.5 – 5 mEq/L)		
Hypokalemia	dysrhythmias and hypotension altered mental status muscle twitching, hypoactive reflexes, or flaccid muscles	acid-base imbalance diarrhea alcoholism Cushing's syndrome

Table 4.7. Electrolyte Imbalances (continued)

Imbalance	Symptoms	Causes
Potassium (normal: 3.5 – 5 mEq/L)		
Hyperkalemia	dysrhythmias or cardiac arrest abdominal cramping and diarrhea anxiety	hemolysis, burns, crushing injury, or rhabdomyolysis decreased urine output
Magnesium (normal: 1.3 – 2.1 mEq/L)		
Hypomagnesemia	dysrhythmias and hypertension seizure hyperreflexia	renal or GI dysfunction diuretic use alcoholism
Hypermagnesemia	dysrhythmias or cardiac arrest bradycardia respiratory depression lethargy/decreased level of consciousness	increased intake renal dysfunction hepatitis Addison's disease
Calcium (normal: 4.5 – 5.5 mEq/L)		
Hypocalcemia	dysrhythmias or cardiac arrest hypotension decreased clotting time seizures	decreased intake renal failure hypoparathyroidism vitamin D deficiency
Hypercalcemia	anxiety and cognitive dysfunction constipation and nausea/vomiting muscle weakness	cancers hyperthyroidism and hyperparathyroidism Paget's disease
Phosphate (normal: 1.8 – 2.3 mEq/L)		
Hypophosphatemia	respiratory distress or failure chest pain seizures decreased level of consciousness increased susceptibility to infection	increased renal excretion
Hyperphosphatemia	tachycardia hyperreflexia soft-tissue calcifications	decreased renal excretion

PATHOLOGIES OF THE RENAL SYSTEM

Urinary tract infections (UTIs) occur when bacteria infects the kidneys, bladder, or urethra. They can occur in men or women but are more common in women. **Pyelonephritis**, infection of the kidneys, occurs when bacteria reach the kidney via the lower urinary tract or the bloodstream.

Chronic kidney disease, in which the kidneys do not function properly for at least three months, can be caused by a number of factors, including diabetes, autoimmune diseases, infections, and drug abuse. People with chronic kidney disease may need dialysis, during which a machine performs the task of the kidneys and removes waste from the blood.

Renal calculi (kidney stones) are hardened mineral deposits that form in the kidneys. They are usually asymptomatic but will cause debilitating pain and urinary symptoms once they pass into the urinary tract.

PRACTICE QUESTIONS

28. Which of the following is the outermost layer of the kidney?
    A) renal cortex
    B) renal medulla
    C) renal pelvis
    D) nephron

29. Which of the following organs holds urine before it passes into the urethra?
    A) prostate
    B) kidney
    C) ureter
    D) urinary bladder

30. Low levels of potassium are most likely to cause which of the following symptoms?
    A) muscle twitching
    B) impaired cognitive functioning
    C) constipation
    D) increased clotting time

The Endocrine System

STRUCTURE AND FUNCTION OF THE ENDOCRINE SYSTEM

The endocrine system is made up of glands that regulate numerous processes throughout the body by secreting chemical messengers called hormones. These hormones regulate a wide variety of bodily processes, including metabolism, growth and development, sexual reproduction, the sleep-wake cycle, and hunger.

The hypothalamus is a gland that plays a central role in the endocrine system by connecting it to the nervous system. Input from the nervous system reaches the hy pothalamus, causing it to release hormones from the pituitary gland. These hormones in turn regulate the release of hormones from many of the other endocrine glands.

HELPFUL HINT

The endocrine system is not directly tested on the exam. However, a basic understanding of hormones will help you better understand how other systems function. For example, the level of calcium (an electrolyte) is regulated by the parathyroid gland.

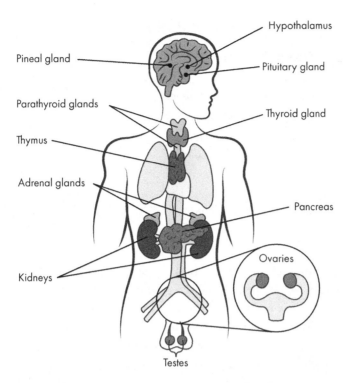

Figure 4.24. The Location of Endocrine Glands

Table 4.8. Endocrine Glands and Their Functions

Gland	Regulates	Hormones Produced
Hypothalamus	pituitary function and metabolic processes including body temperature, hunger, thirst, and circadian rhythms	thyrotropin-releasing hormone (TRH), dopamine, growth hormone–releasing hormone (GHRH), gonadotropin-releasing hormone (GnRH), oxytocin, vaso-pressin
Pituitary gland	growth, blood pressure, reab-sorption of water by the kidneys, temperature, pain relief, and some reproductive functions related to pregnancy and childbirth	human growth hormone (HGH), thyroid-stimulating hormone (TSH), prolactin (PRL), luteinizing hormone (LH), follicle-stimulating hormone (FSH), oxytocin, antidiuretic hormone (ADH)
Pineal gland	circadian rhythms (the sleep-wake cycle)	melatonin
Thyroid gland	energy use and protein synthesis	thyroxine (T_4), triiodothyronine (T_3), calcitonin
Parathyroid	calcium and phosphate levels	parathyroid hormone (PTH)
Adrenal glands	fight-or-flight response and regu-lation of salt and blood volume	epinephrine, norepinephrine, cortisol, androgens
Pancreas	blood sugar levels and metabolism	insulin, glucagon, somatostatin

Table 4.8. Endocrine Glands and Their Functions (continued)

Gland	Regulates	Hormones Produced
Testes	maturation of sex organs, secondary sex characteristics	androgens (e.g., testosterone)
Ovaries	maturation of sex organs, secondary sex characteristics, pregnancy, childbirth, and lactation	progesterone, estrogens
Placenta	gestation and childbirth	progesterone, estrogen, human chorionic gonadotropin, human placental lactogen (hPL)

Many important hormones can be broken down into either anabolic hormones or catabolic hormones. **Anabolic hormones** are associated with the regulation of growth and development; these include testosterone, estrogen, insulin, and human growth hormone. **Catabolic hormones** help regulate the breakdown of substances into smaller molecules. For example, the breakdown of muscle glycogen for energy via the release of **glucagon** is a catabolic process.

PATHOLOGIES OF THE ENDOCRINE SYSTEM

Disruption of hormone production in specific endocrine glands can lead to disease. Overactive or underactive glands can lead to conditions like **hypothyroidism**, which is characterized by a slow metabolism, and **hyperparathyroidism**, which can lead to osteoporosis. **Adrenal insufficiency** (Addison's disease) is the chronic underproduction of steroids.

Diabetes mellitus is a metabolic disorder that affects the body's ability to produce and use **insulin**, a hormone that regulates cellular uptake of glucose (sugar).

- Uncontrolled diabetes can lead to high blood glucose levels (**hyperglycemia**) or low blood glucose levels (**hypoglycemia**).

- **Type 1 diabetes** is an acute-onset autoimmune disease predominant in children, teens, and adults under 30. Beta cells in the pancreas are destroyed and are unable to produce sufficient amounts of insulin, causing blood glucose to rise.

- **Type 2 diabetes** is a gradual-onset disease predominant in adults under 40, but it can develop in individuals of all ages. The person develops insulin resistance, which prevents the cellular uptake of glucose and causes blood glucose to rise. Type 2 diabetes accounts for 90% of all diabetes diagnoses in the United States.

- Diabetes requires long-term management with insulin or oral hypoglycemic drugs.

Thyroid cancer is relatively common but has few or no symptoms. In addition, benign (noncancerous) tumors on the thyroid and other endocrine glands can damage the functioning of a wide variety of bodily systems.

31. Which of the following glands indirectly controls growth by acting on the pituitary gland?

    A) hypothalamus

    B) thyroid gland

    C) adrenal glands

    D) parathyroid glands

32. A patient experiencing symptoms such as kidney stones and arthritis due to a calcium imbalance probably has a disorder of which of the following glands?

    A) hypothalamus

    B) thyroid gland

    C) parathyroid glands

    D) adrenal glands

The Integumentary System
STRUCTURE AND FUNCTION OF THE INTEGUMENTARY SYSTEM

The **integumentary system** refers to the skin (the largest organ in the body) and related structures, including the hair and nails. Skin is composed of three layers. The **epidermis** is the outermost layer of the skin. This waterproof layer contains no blood vessels and acts mainly to protect the body. Under the epidermis lies the **dermis**, which consists of dense connective tissue that allows skin to stretch and flex. The dermis is home to blood vessels, glands, and hair follicles. The **hypodermis** is a layer of fat below the dermis that stores energy (in the form of fat) and acts as a cushion for the body. The hypodermis is sometimes called the **subcutaneous layer**.

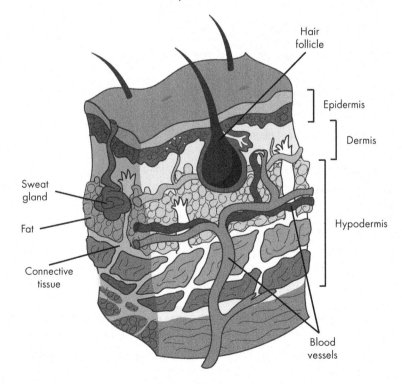

Figure 4.25. The Skin

The skin has several important roles. It acts as a barrier to protect the body from injury, the intrusion of foreign particles, and the loss of water and nutrients. It is also important for **thermoregulation**. Blood vessels near the surface of the skin can dilate, allowing for higher blood flow and the release of heat. They can also constrict to reduce the amount of blood that travels near the surface of the skin, which helps conserve heat. In addition, the skin produces **vitamin D** when exposed to sunlight.

CHECK YOUR UNDER-STANDING

Why would flushing—the reddening of the skin caused by dilating blood vessels—be associated with fevers?

Because the skin covers the whole body, it plays a vital role in allowing organisms to interact with the environment. It is home to nerve endings that sense temperature, pressure, and pain, and it also houses glands that help maintain homeostasis. **Eccrine glands**, which are located primarily in the palms of the hands and soles of the feet (and to a lesser degree in other areas of the body), release the water and salt mixture (sodium chloride, NaCl) called **sweat**. These glands help the body maintain the appropriate salt-water balance. Sweat can also contain small amounts of other substances the body needs to expel, including alcohol, lactic acid, and urea.

Apocrine glands, which are located primarily in the armpit and groin, release an oily substance that contains pheromones. They are also sensitive to adrenaline and are responsible for most of the sweating that occurs due to stress, fear, anxiety, or pain. Apocrine glands are largely inactive until puberty.

PATHOLOGIES OF THE INTEGUMENTARY SYSTEM

Psoriasis is an autoimmune condition that causes inflammation in the skin, resulting in red, flaking patches on the skin. **Eczema** (atopic dermatitis) is a red, itchy rash that usually occurs in children but can occur in adults as well.

Skin cancers can be categorized as melanoma or nonmelanoma cancers. **Melanoma** cancers appear as irregular, dark patches on the skin and are more difficult to treat than nonmelanoma cancers.

PRACTICE QUESTIONS

33. Which of the following is NOT a function of the skin?

A) regulating body temperature

B) protecting against injury

C) producing adrenaline

D) maintaining water-salt balance

34. Which of the following is the outermost layer of the skin?

A) hypodermis

B) dermis

C) epidermis

D) apocrine

HOMEOSTASIS

The human body has many complex systems that maintain **homeostasis**—the body's internal equilibrium. These processes allow the body to monitor external changes and adapt by altering body temperature, blood sugar, blood pressure, and other physiological states.

Feedback mechanisms are the primary forms of communication between the systems working to maintain homeostasis. In a **negative feedback loop**, an external change prompts a response to return the body's internal environmental back to equilibrium. For example, if exposure to heat causes the body's internal temperature to rise, the body will attempt to cool down. Receptors in the skin detect the change in temperature and relay the message to the hypothalamus, which signals sweat glands to release sweat, cooling the body. The process of maintaining homeostasis of internal body temperature is known as **thermoregulation**.

Another example of a negative feedback loop is the regulation of blood glucose levels. When food is consumed, blood glucose levels rise. This rise stimulates the pancreas to produce **insulin**, a hormone that moves glucose into cells, reducing blood glucose levels. When blood glucose is low, the pancreas secretes **glucagon**, a hormone that stimulates production of glucose in the liver. Together, these hormones keep blood glucose in a normal, healthy range.

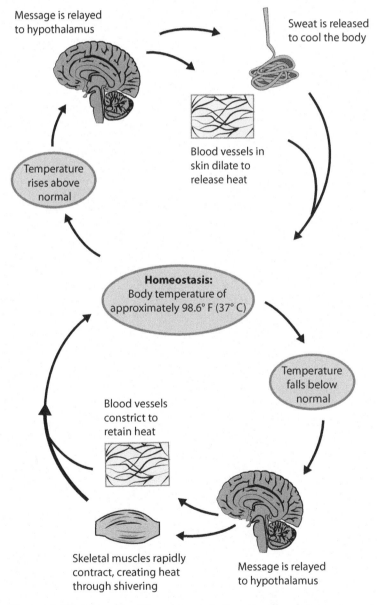

Figure 4.26. Negative Thermoregulation Feedback Loop

Positive feedback loops are not used to maintain homeostasis. Instead, they exacerbate the initial response to a stimulus. Positive feedback loops in the body are rare. One example is the release of oxytocin during childbirth. During labor, the pressure of the fetus on the cervix triggers the release of **oxytocin**, which stimulates uterine contractions. The contractions further increase the pressure on the cervix, resulting in the release of more oxytocin. This cycle continues until the baby is born.

PRACTICE QUESTION

35. Which of the following hormones is replaced when blood glucose levels in the body are too high?

A) insulin

B) oxytocin

C) glucagon

D) thyroxine

Science Review Questions

1. What does the diaphragm do during inspiration?

    A) It relaxes.

    B) It contracts.

    C) It vibrates.

    D) It expands.

2. How many bones comprise the thoracic vertebrae?

    A) 5

    B) 7

    C) 12

    D) 33

3. Which of the following describes the biceps when the elbow is flexed?

    A) antagonist

    B) agonist

    C) fixator

    D) synergist

4. Which part of a nerve cell holds the cellular organelles?

    A) soma

    B) dendrite

    C) axon

    D) synapse

5. Which digestive enzyme breaks down fat molecules into monoglycerides and fatty acids?

    A) pancreatic amylase

    B) trypsin

    C) pancreatic lipase

    D) chymotrypsin

6. In which part of the kidneys are the collecting ducts located?

    A) renal cortex

    B) renal medulla

    C) renal pelvis

    D) renal calculus

7. Which blood vessels are closest to the cells of the body, making the exchange of nutrients, gases, and cellular waste possible?

    A) veins

    B) arteries

    C) capillaries

    D) venules

8. Which of the following refers to the large amount of air moved during a deep breath?

    A) vital signs

    B) vital capacity

    C) vital volume

    D) vital respiration

9. Which of the following is the largest bone in the human body?

    A) femur

    B) humerus

    C) scapula

    D) tibia

10. Which of the following describes the triceps when the elbow is extended?

   A) agonist

   B) antagonist

   C) fixator

   D) synergist

11. Which of the following surrounds neurons and provides protection?

   A) dendrite

   B) axon

   C) neuron

   D) neuroglia

12. The digestive enzymes produced by the pancreas pass into which organ?

   A) stomach

   B) gall bladder

   C) large intestine

   D) small intestine

13. What structure drains the urine into the bladder?

   A) ureter

   B) urethra

   C) nephron

   D) glomerulus

14. What is the relationship between the pressure in the lungs and the movement of air out of the lungs?

   A) Negative pressure in the lungs moves the air out.

   B) Positive pressure in the lungs moves the air out.

   C) Neutral pressure in the lungs moves the air out.

   D) Decreasing pressure in the lungs moves the air out.

15. Which of the following is a sesamoid bone?

   A) hip bone

   B) sacrum

   C) patella

   D) sternum

16. Which of the following protects the spinal cord?

   A) rib cage

   B) vertebral cavity

   C) sternal notch

   D) pelvic cavity

17. Which lobe of the liver spirals around the inferior vena cava?

   A) left

   B) right

   C) caudate

   D) quadrate

18. Which of the following is true about air in the lungs?

   A) During expiration, air completely leaves the lungs.

   B) There is always about a liter of air in the lungs.

   C) Shallow breathing does not circulate any air through the lungs.

   D) Deep breathing moves a maximum of two liters of air through the lungs.

19. Which of the following bones are directly connected to the ulna and radius?

   A) carpal

   B) metacarpal

   C) tarsal

   D) metatarsal

20. Which of the following is the outer and most durable layer of the meninges?

   A) pia mater

   B) dura mater

   C) arachnoid mater

   D) subarachnoid space

21. Serosa, one of the layers of the stomach, secretes a serous fluid. What is the function of this fluid?

   A) It protects the stomach from the acidity of its contents.

   B) It prevents friction from the organs around the stomach.

   C) It enables the stomach to stretch and relax.

   D) It maintains a moist environment in the stomach.

22. Which of the following are the hollow spaces in the brain that are filled with cerebrospinal fluid?

   A) canals

   B) sacs

   C) ventricles

   D) pouches

23. Sphincters close and open to prevent entry or escape of a substance. Which of the following does not have a sphincter?

   A) bladder

   B) esophagus

   C) nares

   D) capillaries

24. Which of the following bones is part of the vertebral column?

   A) coccyx

   B) hyoid

   C) sternum

   D) clavicle

25. Which of following best describes the function of white matter?

   A) It gathers signals from the sensory organs.

   B) It protects the brain from injury.

   C) It transmits information between regions of the brain.

   D) It secretes hormones that regulate the nervous system.

1. **A) is correct.** The meninges are connective tissue.

2. **D) is correct.** The mitochondria found in cells are what power the cell and provide it with the energy it needs to carry out its life functions. Muscle cells need a lot of ATP in order to provide the energy needed for movement and exercise.

3. **A) is correct.** The wrist is distal, or further from the trunk, relative to the elbow.

4. **C) is correct.** The abdominal cavity holds organs involved in urinary and digestive function, including the appendix.

5. **B) is correct.** Red blood cells (RBCs) carry oxygen throughout the body so it can be absorbed into cells and used for cellular respiration. Oxygen is carried on hemoglobin, an iron-containing protein found in RBCs.

6. **A) is correct.** People with von Willebrand disease will bleed easily and for longer periods of time. Symptoms range from easy bruising and nosebleeds to life-threatening hemorrhages following trauma or surgery.

7. **A) is correct.** The myocardium is the muscular layer of the heart that contains cardiac muscle.

8. **D) is correct.** The right ventricle pumps deoxygenated blood from the heart to the lungs.

9. **D) is correct.** Blood leaves the heart in arteries.

10. **D) is correct.** The epiglottis covers the esophagus during respiration so that air does not enter the digestive track.

11. **C) is correct.** The alveoli are sacs found at the terminal end of each bronchiole in the lungs and are the site of gas exchange with the blood.

12. **C) is correct.** Asthma is a negative reaction of the body to otherwise harmless particles.

13. **B) is correct.** The axon carries information away from the soma, or body of the cell.

14. **B) is correct.** The somatic nervous system controls voluntary actions.

15. **A) is correct.** Schwann cells secrete myelin, which forms a sheet around the neuron and allows the electrical signal to travel faster.

16. **A) is correct.** Stem cells are found in red bone marrow.

17. **A) is correct.** Long bones are the main bones composing the arms and legs.

18. **C) is correct.** Calcium is released as bones are degraded, which helps balance the calcium level in the body.

19. **B) is correct.** Blood is moved through blood vessels by visceral, or smooth, muscle that cannot be voluntarily controlled.

20. **D) is correct.** Myofibrils are the muscle fibers that contract.

21. **D) is correct.** A muscle strain is caused by the overstretching of muscle fibers, resulting in tearing of the muscle.

22. **C) is correct.** Antibodies are part of the body's adaptive immune system and only respond to specific pathogens.

23. **B) is correct.** Inflammation increases the blood flow to the damaged area, increasing its temperature and bringing white blood cells to the site.

24. **C) is correct.** Monocytes use phagocytosis to "swallow" and break down pathogens.

25. **D) is correct.** The liver is an accessory organ of the gastrointestinal system: it produces fluids that aid in digestion, but food does not pass through it.

26. **A) is correct.** Most nutrients are absorbed by the small intestine.

27. **A) is correct.** The liver produces bile, which is needed for the digestion of fats.

28. **A) is correct.** The outermost layer of the kidney is the renal cortex.

29. **D) is correct.** The urinary bladder holds urine before it passes to the urethra to be excreted.

30. **A) is correct.** Cells need potassium to transmit the nerve impulses that cause muscle contraction. Low potassium interferes with this process, leading to muscle twitching.

31. **A) is correct.** The hypothalamus releases hormones that in turn cause the pituitary gland to release growth-related hormones.

32. **C) is correct.** The parathyroid glands regulate levels of calcium and phosphate in the body.

33. **C) is correct.** The skin does not produce adrenaline. (Adrenaline is produced and released by the adrenal glands.)

34. **C) is correct.** The epidermis is the outermost layer of the skin. It is waterproof and does not contain any blood vessels.

35. **A) is correct.** When blood glucose levels rise, the body release insulin to move glucose into cells and lower blood glucose levels.

1. **B) is correct.** The diaphragm contracts during inspiration, or inhalation, to provide space for air to move into the lungs.

2. **C) is correct.** There are twelve bones in the thoracic, or chest, vertebrae.

3. **B) is correct.** When the elbow is flexed, the biceps is contracted while the triceps is relaxed. Thus, the biceps is the agonist while the triceps is the antagonist.

4. **A) is correct.** The soma houses the cellular organelles.

5. **C) is correct.** Pancreatic lipase is responsible for breaking down fat molecules into monoglycerides and fatty acids.

6. **B) is correct.** The collecting ducts are located in the renal medulla.

7. **C) is correct.** Capillaries enable the exchange of nutrients, gases, and waste on the cellular level.

8. **B) is correct.** Vital capacity is the large amount of air that is moved during deep breathing.

9. **A) is correct.** The femur, or thigh bone, is the largest bone in the human body.

10. **A) is correct.** The triceps is the agonist; it contracts to extend the elbow.

11. **D) is correct.** The neuroglia protects the neuron by surrounding it.

12. **D) is correct.** The digestive enzymes produced by the pancreas pass into the small intestine.

13. **A) is correct.** Urine passes through the ureters from the kidneys into the urinary bladder.

14. **B) is correct.** Positive pressure in the lungs will move air out of the lungs.

15. **C) is correct.** The patella, or kneecap, is a sesamoid bone attached to the tendon of the quadriceps.

16. **B) is correct.** The vertebral cavity protects the spinal cord.

17. **C) is correct.** The caudate lobe spirals around the vena cava while the quadrate lobe is located around the gallbladder.

18. **B) is correct.** The lungs will never be absent of air, even during expiration.

19. **A) is correct.** The eight carpal bones are in the wrist and connect the bones of the forearm (ulna and radius) to the hand.

20. **B) is correct.** Dura mater is the outermost layer of the meninges, which protect the spinal cord and brain.

21. **B) is correct.** The serous fluid keeps the outside of the stomach wet, preventing friction with the organs close to it.

22. **C) is correct.** Ventricles are the hollow spaces in the brain where cerebrospinal fluid can be found.

23. **C) is correct.** The nares (nostrils) do not have sphincters and are always open.

24. **A) is correct.** The coccyx is located at the tip of the vertebral column.

25. **C) is correct.** White matter is composed of myelinated neurons that carry information between regions of the brain.

FIVE: PRACTICE TEST

Reading

Directions: Read the passage, and then answer the questions that follow.

The following passage refers to questions 1–6.

The endocrine system is made up of glands—such as the parathyroid, thyroid, pituitary, and adrenals—that produce hormones. Men and women have different reproductive glands: men have testes and women have ovaries. The pituitary gland serves as the "master gland" of the endocrine system.

The endocrine system's function is to produce and distribute hormones. Endocrine glands release hormones into the bloodstream, where they are carried to other tissues or organs. When the hormones reach other tissues, they catalyze certain chemical reactions, stimulating various processes or activities. For instance, hormones are responsible for important bodily processes such as puberty and menstruation. Hormones are also released in humans in moments of fear or anxiety and can trigger the fight-or-flight response. The endocrine system is the primary source of a wide range of physiological activities and is sometimes referred to as the "hardworking chemical control center" of the human body.

1. What is the author's primary purpose in writing this essay?

   A) to warn people about the dangers of hormonal imbalance

   B) to persuade people to take care of their endocrine glands

   C) to advise people about different hormones and what they do

   D) to inform people about the endocrine system's parts and functions

2. Which of the following statements can be considered a statement of FACT according to the content offered in the paragraphs above?

   A) The endocrine system is the most important system in the human body.

   B) The endocrine system is the only "chemical control center in the body."

   C) The endocrine system only has one organ: the pancreas.

   D) The endocrine system stimulates reactions in the body by releasing hormones.

3. What is the best summary of the passage?

   A) The endocrine system controls hormones that stimulate processes in the body.

   B) Endocrine glands differ in men and women.

   C) The pituitary gland is the "master gland" of the endocrine system.

   D) Hormones are responsible for puberty and menstruation.

4. According to the passage, what is true about hormones?

   A) They are only secreted by the pancreas.

   B) They can help trigger fight-or-flight responses.

   C) They almost always cause negative reactions.

   D) Their sole purpose is to stimulate reproductive activities.

5. According to the passage, what serves as the major organ associated with the endocrine system?

   A) the pituitary gland

   B) the testicles

   C) the ovaries

   D) the spinal cord

6. What is the meaning of the word *stimulating* in the second paragraph?

   A) to make something happen

   B) to reproduce something

   C) to create fear or anxiety

   D) to destroy or diminish a tissue

The following passage refers to questions 7–12.

Every medical professional should understand the root causes and potential effects of hypoglycemia because it can actually be a matter of life or death for a patient with diabetes. Hypoglycemia—which literally means low (*hypo*) blood sugar (*glycemia*)—is one of the most common medical emergencies for patients who have diabetes. Hypoglycemia can occur when a patient either takes too much insulin or has not consumed enough sugar. At other times, hypoglycemia stems from overexertion. A person can even become hypoglycemic if they vomit an important meal, depriving the body of the sugar and nutrients it needs to stay balanced.

Any medical professional interacting with diabetic patients should know the telltale signs of hypoglycemia. When a diabetic patient's blood sugar plummets, their mental state becomes altered. This can lead to unconsciousness or, in more severe cases, a diabetic coma and/or brain damage. If you notice the rapid onset of nervousness or anxiety, shakiness, and/or profuse sweating in someone with diabetes, you will likely need to help administer glucose to them as soon as possible (as long as they are conscious enough to swallow). Most diabetic patients manage their condition by using glucometers.

Glucometers measure the level of glucose in the bloodstream. During a potential hypoglycemic episode, if at all possible, ask the person if they have used their glucometer lately or encourage them to use it immediately. If the person is still cognizant but looks "out of it," you may have to assist in the process. A blood glucose value of less than 80 milligrams per deciliter can be considered a hypoglycemic episode. This kind of reading would prompt a swift glucose administration and, in worst-case scenarios, a trip to the emergency room.

7. What is the main idea of the passage?

   A) Medical professionals should know what causes hypoglycemia and how to manage it.

   B) Glucometers help patients with diabetes monitor their glucose levels.

   C) Patients with diabetes can slip into a diabetic coma if they do not monitor their glucose levels.

   D) Profuse sweating is one of the most telltale signs of a hypoglycemic episode.

8. What is the meaning of the word *administer* in the second paragraph?

   A) adorn

   B) give

   C) revive

   D) withdraw

9. Which of the following is NOT listed as a detail in the passage?

   A) Glucometers help patients and medical professionals measure the level of glucose in the bloodstream.

   B) Any blood glucose value that reads less than 80 milligrams per deciliter can be considered a hypoglycemic episode.

   C) Only people with diabetes can become hypoglycemic.

   D) Hypoglycemia literally means low (*hypo*) blood sugar (*glycemia*).

10. What is the author's primary purpose in writing this essay?

    A) to inform health care workers and the public about the symptoms of hypoglycemia and how to respond to it

    B) to persuade people to purchase more glucometers so that they can properly handle all hypoglycemic episodes

    C) to dramatize a hypoglycemic episode so readers will know what to expect if they encounter a patient with diabetes who is undergoing one

    D) to recount a time when a medical professional failed to properly respond to a hypoglycemic episode

11. Which of the following statements is a fact stated in the passage?

    A) Profuse sweating is the number one sign that tells a medical professional a hypoglycemic episode has concluded.

    B) Any blood glucose value that reads less than 80 milligrams per deciliter can be considered a hypoglycemic episode.

    C) Most diabetic patients do not know how to monitor their own condition, so health care workers must help them.

    D) Most personal glucometers are outdated, and medical professionals should purchase their own.

12. Which of the following statements can the reader infer from the passage?

    A) Diabetic comas, which can be triggered by untreated episodes of hypoglycemia, can cause permanent brain damage.

    B) Glucometers are too expensive for most diabetic patients to purchase, making cases of hypoglycemia frequent.

    C) Medical professionals should ignore the personal perspectives of people experiencing hypoglycemic episodes.

    D) Diabetes is a dangerous disease that cannot be managed properly.

The following passage refers to questions 13–18.

Communicating with any human being in crisis—whether that crisis is physical or emotional—is going to be more difficult than normal, everyday communication. Thus, emergency responders and medical practitioners, like many other social service providers, need to learn how to be sensitive in interpersonal communication. Here are some tips about how to hone your craft as a communicator while working with people in crisis. These tips can also be used for everyday communication.

First, it is essential that you are aware of cultural differences. In some cultures, direct eye contact can be unsettling or disrespectful. People from different cultures may have different comfort levels with personal space: some might find physical closeness comforting; others might find it threatening. Your body language speaks volumes. Be sure you are aware of the symbolic nature of your posture, hand motions, and gestures.

It is also important to enunciate your verbal statements and directions in a clear, relevant way. Use terminology and directions that a patient will understand, and avoid lofty medical jargon. Believe it or not, you also want to be honest with the person in crisis, even if the conditions are dire. Also explain, if possible, what you might do to help alleviate even the most drastic conditions so that the person feels supported. Lastly, and most importantly, be prepared to listen. Even if there is a language barrier, condition, or disability limiting your communication with the person in crisis, try to position yourself as an active listener. These tips will help you support people who need clarity and sensitivity.

13. What is the best summary of the passage?

    A) In some cultures, direct eye contact can be unsettling or disrespectful.

    B) Posture, hand motions, and gestures can symbolize respect or disrespect.

    C) Medical practitioners must learn to be sensitive with people who are in crisis.

    D) Medical practitioners should give clear directions and avoid using lofty medical jargon.

14. What is the author's primary purpose in writing this essay?

    A) to warn people about the dangers of disrespectful communication

    B) to persuade medical personnel to speak only when it is necessary

    C) to tell an interesting story about a paramedic who offended a patient

    D) to advise medical practitioners about communicating with patients in crisis

15. According to the passage, what is true about cultural differences?

    A) People from most cultures can recognize a thumbs-up gesture.

    B) In some cultures, people are uncomfortable with direct eye contact.

    C) When a crisis occurs, cultural differences usually disappear.

    D) No matter what someone's culture is, everyone needs a hug in a crisis.

16. Which of the following statements can be considered a statement of FACT according to the content offered in the paragraphs above?

    A) Most people cannot handle it if you look them in the eye and tell "dire" truths.

    B) Communicating with someone in crisis is more difficult than normal communication.

    C) The most important part of sensitive communication is establishing physical contact.

    D) Communicating with patients is not as important as dealing quickly with their injuries.

17. According to the passage, what do most people in crisis need?

    A) medical care

    B) psychological counseling

    C) cultural understanding

    D) sensitivity and clarity

18. What is the meaning of the phrase "speaks volumes" in the second paragraph?

    A) talks too much

    B) reads instructions

    C) communicates many things

    D) reads novels in several volumes

The following passage refers to questions 19–22.

Empathy is different from mimicry or sympathy—it is neither imitating someone else's emotions nor feeling concern for their suffering. Empathy is much more complex; it is the ability to actually share and comprehend the emotions of others.

Empathy takes on two major forms: cognitive empathy and affective, or emotional, empathy. Cognitive empathy is the ability to identify and understand the emotions, mental state, or perspective of others. Affective empathy is the ability to experience an emotional response to the emotions of others—either to feel what they are feeling or to have an appropriate emotional reaction, such as feeling sad when hearing about someone's bad news. Related to affective empathy is compassionate empathy, the ability to control your own emotions while helping others deal with theirs.

Empathy is crucial for being able to respond properly in social settings. People who suffer from some psychiatric conditions, such as autism spectrum disorder, may struggle with being empathetic. Conversely, some people with very strong cognitive empathy may abuse their social understanding as a means to take advantage of others. Most people, however, choose moments and contexts in which they are likely to relate to the emotions of others.

19. The reader can infer from the passage that the author believes empathy is

   A) a primarily positive quality.

   B) similar to autism spectrum disorder.

   C) similar to mimicry or sympathy.

   D) a good quality is some cases and a bad quality in others.

20. What is the author's primary purpose in writing these paragraphs?

   A) to define empathy

   B) to persuade readers to show more empathy

   C) to advise readers about ways to appear empathetic

   D) to show that empathy is a better quality than sympathy

21. Which qualities can readers infer might be most useful to a medical professional who responds to emergencies?

   A) sympathy and mimicry

   B) cognitive empathy

   C) affective empathy

   D) compassionate empathy

22. According to the passage, what is one negative use of empathy?

   A) People who actually possess little or no empathy may fake this quality.

   B) People who are empathetic may feel too much concern for others' suffering.

   C) People with affective empathy may experience an emotional response to others' emotions.

   D) People who are able to identify and understand others' emotions, mental state, or perspective may abuse this knowledge by taking advantage of others.

Writing

Directions: Read the passage, and then answer the questions that follow.

The following passage refers to questions 1–3.

(1) Have you ever devoured a tasty snow cone only to experience the agony of a "brain freeze"? (2) Have you ever wondered why or how that happens? (3) Well, scientists now believe they understand the mechanism of these so-called ice cream headaches.

(4) It begins with the icy temperature of the snow cone (or any cold food, or sometimes even exposure to cold air). (5) When a cold substance (delicious or otherwise) presses against the roof of your mouth, it causes blood vessels there to begin constricting, and your body starts to sense that something is awry. (6) In response, blood is pumped to the affected region to try to warm it up, causing rapid dilation of the same vessels. (7) This causes the neighboring trigeminal nerve to send rapid signals to your brain. (8) Because the trigeminal nerve also serves the face. (9) The brain misinterprets these signals as coming from your forehead.

(10) Regardless of the time spent wincing, the danger of the ice cream headache that certainly will not stop people for screaming for their favorite frozen treat in the future.

1. Which sentence in the second paragraph is missing an independent clause?

 A) sentence 5

 B) sentence 6

 C) sentence 7

 D) sentence 8

2. Which sentence contains an extra word?

 A) sentence 7, "to"

 B) sentence 8, "also"

 C) sentence 9, "as"

 D) sentence 10, "that"

3. Where is the best place to add this sentence?

 The duration of the pain varies from a few seconds up to about a minute.

 A) after sentence 3

 B) after sentence 4

 C) after sentence 9

 D) after sentence 10

The following passage refers to questions 4 and 5.

(1) The word *bacteria* typically conjures images of disease-inducing invaders that attack our immune systems. (2) However, recent research is changing that perception. (3) Plenty of scholarly articles point to the benefits of healthy bacteria that actually reinforce the immune system. (4) According to new research, the "microbiome"—that the resident bacteria in your digestive system—may impact your health in multiple ways. (5) Scientists who been studying microbial DNA now believe that internal bacteria can influence metabolism, mental health, and mood. (6) Some even suggest that imbalances in your digestive microbiome correlate with disorders like obesity and autoimmune diseases.

4. Which sentence contains an unnecessary word?

 A) sentence 1, "that"

 B) sentence 2, "that"

 C) sentence 3, "that"

 D) sentence 4, "that"

5. Which sentence has a verb error?

 A) sentence 3

 B) sentence 4

 C) sentence 5

 D) sentence 6

The following passage refers to questions 6 and 7.

(1) We all know how vital blood is for the human body—it transports oxygen from our lungs, removes waste from our organs, and protects our bodies from infections. (2) Blood feeds and stimulate the neurological processes of the nervous system. (3) It pumps waste products through the liver and kidneys of the excretory system. (4) It even releases antibodies so the immune system can help destroy potentially harmful microorganisms in the body. (5) Blood is one of the most versatile components of human life.

6. Where is the best place to add this sentence?

It plays an integral part in the processes of all other systems in the human body.

A) after sentence 1

B) after sentence 2

C) after sentence 3

D) after sentence 5

7. Which sentence has a verb error?

A) sentence 1

B) sentence 2

C) sentence 3

D) sentence 4

The following passage refers to questions 8–10.

(1) Across the globe, women are, on average, outliving their male counterparts. (2) Although this gender gap has shrunk over the last decade thanks to medical improvements and lifestyle changes, women are still expected to live four and a half years longer than men. (3) What are the reason for this trend? (4) The answer may lie in our sex hormones.

(5) Men are more likely to exhibit riskier behaviors than women, especially between the ages of fifteen and twenty-four, when testosterone production is at its peak. (6) Testosterone is correlated with aggressive and reckless behaviors that contribute to high mortality rates—think road rage, alcohol consumption, drug use, and smoking.

(7) Estrogen, on the other hand, seems to be correlated with cholesterol levels: an increase in estrogen is accompanied by a decrease in "bad" cholesterol, which may confer advantages by reducing the risk of heart attack and stroke.

(8) Of course, lifestyle and diet are also components of this difference in life expectancy. (9) Men are more likely to be involved in more physically dangerous jobs, such as manufacturing or construction. (10) They may be less likely to eat as many fruits and vegetables as their female counterparts. (11) And may be more likely to consume more red meat, including processed meat. (12) Better health decisions and better nutrition may eventually even the score in men's and women's life expectancy.

8. Which sentence contains a verb error?

A) sentence 1

B) sentence 2

C) sentence 3

D) sentence 4

9. Which sentence is missing a subject?

A) sentence 8

B) sentence 9

C) sentence 10

D) sentence 11

10. Where is the best place to add this sentence?

These types of meats have been linked to high cholesterol, hypertension, and cancer.

A) after sentence 7

B) after sentence 8

C) after sentence 11

D) after sentence 12

The following passage refers to questions 11–13.

(1) Autism is a psychiatric condition that exists along a spectrum ranging from mild to severe. (2) It affects communication, social interaction, and behavior. (3) People with severe cases of autism is likely to be unable to communicate verbally or nonverbally. (4) They do not initiate social interactions and may be unable to respond appropriately when spoken to. (5) They often engage in repetitive behaviors.

(6) On the other hand, people at the mild end of the spectrum may appear to have good social skills, making their condition less likely to be detected. (7) However, they may struggle with social situations. (8) They may have to be taught to make eye contact and how to engage in back-and-forth conversation with friends, peers, teachers, employers, and others. (9) And may have extremely focused interests and require routines to stay on an even keel.

(10) There is not a one-size-fits-all way to interact with people with autism spectrum disorder, so it is best for teachers, employers, coworkers, and friends to collaborate with these unique learners on a case-by-case basis.

11. Which sentence contains a verb error?

   A) sentence 1

   B) sentence 2

   C) sentence 3

   D) sentence 4

12. Which sentence is missing a subject?

   A) sentence 6

   B) sentence 7

   C) sentence 8

   D) sentence 9

13. Where is the best place to add this sentence?

People at this end of the spectrum need lifelong support.

   A) after sentence 4

   B) after sentence 5

   C) after sentence 6

   D) after sentence 7

The following passage refers to questions 14 and 15.

(1) A variety of environmental factors can inhibit the body's ability to naturally keep itself cool. (2) On the other hand, extremely dry heat may encourage people to push beyond their normal boundaries of exertion because they do not "feel" the heat as much as in humid environments. (3) Overexertion in either moist or dry heat forces the body to alter its heat-coping mechanisms, placing people at risk of experiencing heat cramps, heat exhaustion, or heat stroke. (4) These physiological responses to heat exposure can impair important bodily functions and can even result in death.

(5) Heat cramps occur when an excessive amount of water and salts are released from the body—in the form of sweat—in hot conditions. (6) Prolonged loss of water and salts will lead to muscle cramps, usually in the legs or abdomen. (7) Excessive loss of fluids and salts can also lead to heat exhaustion, a state in which a person experiences shallow breathing, an altered mental state, unresponsiveness, dizziness or faintness, and/or moist and cool skin. (8) These symptoms occur as a result of circulatory dysfunction. (9) The overexposure to heat combined with the loss of fluids disrupted normal blood flow.

14. Which sentence contains a verb error?

   A) sentence 6

   B) sentence 7

   C) sentence 8

   D) sentence 9

15. Where is the best place to add this sentence?

Humid conditions, for instance, mean that sweat evaporates slowly, reducing the body's ability to radiate heat.

A) after sentence 1

B) after sentence 2

C) after sentence 3

D) after sentence 4

The following passage refers to questions 16 and 17.

(1) Inflammation is one of the body's most vital forms of defense. (2) But can also be detrimental if it does not "turn off" or if it rushes to the aid of otherwise healthy tissue. (3) Inflammatory diseases like inflammatory bowel disease (IBD) or rheumatoid arthritis can have debilitating effects. (4) Chronic inflammation can cause pain, fatigue, gastrointestinal problems, and other symptoms. (5) Anti-inflammatory medications and certain steroids can lessen the inflammation and relieved some of the symptoms.

16. Which sentence is missing a subject?

A) sentence 1

B) sentence 2

C) sentence 3

D) sentence 4

17. Which sentence has a verb error?

A) sentence 2

B) sentence 3

C) sentence 4

D) sentence 5

The following passage refers to questions 18 and 19.

(1) Hormone feedback systems can involve steroid hormones. (2) For example, testosterone is a steroid hormone that influences male secondary sexual characteristics that develop during puberty. (3) Its level is influenced by the production of follicle-stimulating hormone (FSH) and luteinizing hormone (LH) in a negative feedback loop. (4) When testosterone reaches a certain level, it inhibits the production of FSH and LH. (5) As testosterone levels fall, FSH and LH begin to be released again, starting the cycle over. (6) A similar but more complex feedback loop occurs in women with FSH and LH stimulating the production of estrogen. (7) Resulting in the cycle of ovulation and menstruation.

18. Where is the best place to add this sentence?

The release of FSH and LH stimulates the production of testosterone.

A) after sentence 1

B) after sentence 2

C) after sentence 3

D) after sentence 4

19. Which sentence contains a grammar error?

A) sentence 4

B) sentence 5

C) sentence 6

D) sentence 7

The following passage refers to questions 20 and 21.

(1) In 2016, President Barack Obama's administration released its national dietary guidelines, which featured some changes from earlier versions. (2) While previous national guidelines focused on the dangers of cholesterol; the Obama administration's new guidelines highlighted the dangers of processed sugar. (3) According to the guidelines, sugar should account for no more than 10 percent of a healthy adult's total daily calories, or about 200 calories. (4)

Obama's guidelines warning against the dangers of "empty calories" such as those from soft drinks. (5) In particular, the guidelines called for an increased awareness of sugar consumption among men, who are disproportionately affected by excessive sugar intake. (6) They urged men to eat more vegetables and foods with fiber to help stave off health risks like heart disease, colon cancer, hypertension, stroke, and diabetes, some of which are directly correlated with the overconsumption of sugar.

20. Which sentence contains a punctuation error?

A) sentence 1

B) sentence 2

C) sentence 3

D) sentence 4

21. Which sentence contains a verb error?

A) sentence 3

B) sentence 4

C) sentence 5

D) sentence 6

Mathematics

Directions: Work the problem, and then choose the correct answer.

1. A pharmacy technician fills 13 prescriptions in 30 minutes. At that rate, how many prescriptions can he fill in a 7-hour shift?

A) 91

B) 45

C) 182

D) 208

2. A patient weighs 110 pounds. What is her weight in kilograms?

A) 55 kg

B) 50 kg

C) 11 kg

D) 20 kg

3. A patient has a condition that requires her to limit her fluid intake to 1800 milliliters per day. A family member brings her a bottle of water that contains 591 milliliters, and she drinks the whole bottle. How many milliliters of water can the patient ingest the rest of the day?

A) 1391 ml

B) 1209 ml

C) 2391 ml

D) 1309 ml

4. Andre welded together three pieces of metal pipe, measuring 26.5 inches, 18.9 inches, and 35.1 inches. How long was the welded pipe?

A) 10.3 in

B) 80.5 in

C) 27.5 in

D) 42.7 in

5. A doctor advises her prediabetic patient to decrease his sugar consumption by 25%. If he currently consumes 40 grams of sugar per day on average, how many grams of sugar per day should he have now?

A) 10 g

B) 16 g

C) 24 g

D) 30 g

6. In its first year of business, a small company lost $2100. The next year, the company recorded a profit of $11,200. What was the company's average profit over the two years?

A) $5650

B) $4550

C) $9100

D) $11,300

7. Bob's hospital bill is $1896. If Bob pays $158 per month, which expression represents his balance after x months?

A) $158(1896 - x)$

B) $158x + 1896$

C) $1738x$

D) $1896 - 158x$

8. The dosage for a certain medication is 2 milligrams per kilogram. What dosage should be given to a patient weighing 165 pounds?

A) 150 mg

B) 250 mg

C) 132 mg

D) 50 mg

9. The ratio of men to women in a nursing program is 2 to 7. If there are 72 men in the program, how many women are there?

    A) 504 women

    B) 21 women

    C) 252 women

    D) 210 women

10. A doctor has prescribed Norco 10/325, which contains 10 milligrams of hydrocodone and 325 milligrams of acetaminophen , to help control a patient's post-op pain. The warning on the prescription label cautions patients to limit their intake of acetaminophen to less than 3500 milligrams per day. How many tablets can the patient take while staying under the daily limit?

    A) 9

    B) 10

    C) 11

    D) 12

11. Chris makes $13.50 an hour. How much will he earn in a 7.5-hour day?

    A) $101.25

    B) $1012.50

    C) $20.75

    D) $91.00

12. How much alcohol by volume is in a 500 milliliter bottle of 70% isopropyl alcohol?

    A) 35 ml

    B) 50 ml

    C) 400 ml

    D) 350 ml

13. Rosie has $145. She needs to buy a new dishwasher that costs $520. How much will she need to save each week to be able to buy the dishwasher in five weeks?

    A) $75

    B) $80

    C) $104

    D) $133

14. The average high temperature in Paris, France, in July is 25°C. Convert the temperature to Fahrenheit.

    A) 13°F

    B) 43°F

    C) 77°F

    D) 57°F

15. The recommended dosage of a particular medication is 4 milliliters per 50 pounds of body weight. What is the recommended dosage for a person who weighs 175 pounds?

    A) 25 ml

    B) 140 ml

    C) 14 ml

    D) 28 ml

16. A medication's expiration date has passed. The label says it contains 600 milligrams of ibuprofen, but it has lost 125 milligrams of ibuprofen. How much ibuprofen is left in the tablet?

    A) 475 mg

    B) 525 mg

    C) 425 mg

    D) 125 mg

17. Dashawn is baking two desserts for Thanksgiving dinner. One recipe calls for $2\frac{1}{2}$ cups of flour and the other recipe calls for $1\frac{1}{3}$ cups of flour. If the flour canister had 8 cups of flour before he started baking, how much flour is left?

A) $4\frac{3}{5}$ c

B) $5\frac{5}{6}$ c

C) $4\frac{1}{6}$ c

D) $5\frac{2}{5}$ c

18. A hospital delivered 2213 babies last year, and 44% of those babies were boys. How many boys were born in that hospital last year? Round the answer to the nearest whole number.

A) 1239 boys

B) 1170 boys

C) 974 boys

D) 503 boys

19. If the average person drinks ten 8-ounce glasses of water each day, how many ounces of water will she drink in a week?

A) 80 oz

B) 700 oz

C) 560 oz

D) 70 oz

20. If one serving of milk contains 280 milligrams of calcium, how much calcium is in 1.5 servings?

A) 187 mg

B) 295 mg

C) 420 mg

D) 200 mg

21. Solve: $5(x + 3) - 12 = 43$

A) 8

B) 12

C) 9

D) 10

22. Normal body temperature is 98.6°F. Convert the temperature to Celsius.

A) 37°C

B) 54.8°C

C) 66.6°C

D) 47°C

23. Alice ran $3\frac{1}{2}$ miles on Monday, and she increased her distance by $\frac{1}{4}$ mile each day. What was her total distance from Monday to Friday?

A) $17\frac{1}{2}$ mi

B) 20 mi

C) $18\frac{1}{2}$ mi

D) 19 mi

24. An expired medication originally contained 500 milligrams of the active ingredient, but the content is now 150 milligrams. What percent of the active ingredient has been lost?

A) 30%

B) 70%

C) 35%

D) 50%

25. Jack missed 5% of 260 work days last year, some for illness and some for vacation. How many days did Jack work?

A) 13 days

B) 208 days

C) 247 days

D) 255 days

26. Fried's rule for computing an infant's dose of medication is:

$$\frac{\text{child's age in months} \times \text{adult dosage}}{150}$$

If the adult dose is 25 milligrams, how much should be given to a one-and-a-half-year-old child?

A) 3 mg

B) 6 mg

C) 4 mg

D) 5 mg

27. A carpenter is planning to add wood trim along three sides of a doorway. The sides of the doorway measure $7\frac{1}{2}$ feet, $2\frac{5}{8}$ feet, and $7\frac{1}{2}$ feet. How much wood trim is needed?

A) $16\frac{5}{8}$ ft

B) $17\frac{5}{8}$ ft

C) $16\frac{1}{2}$ ft

D) $17\frac{1}{2}$ ft

28. Kenna lost an average of 1.1 pounds per week for an entire year. How much weight did she lose? (Round to the nearest whole number.)

A) 47 lb

B) 53 lb

C) 46 lb

D) 58 lb

Science

Directions: Read the question, and then choose the most correct answer.

1. Which of the following types of cell carries hemoglobin in the blood?

   A) white blood cell

   B) red blood cell

   C) platelet

   D) T cell

2. The incus, stapes, and malleus play an important role in which sense?

   A) vision

   B) taste

   C) hearing

   D) smell

3. Which of the following is released when bone is broken down?

   A) phosphorous

   B) iron

   C) calcium

   D) zinc

4. Which chamber of the heart pumps deoxygenated blood to the lungs?

   A) right atrium

   B) right ventricle

   C) left atrium

   D) left ventricle

5. Which of the following is the network of capillaries in the kidneys where filtration begins?

   A) renal pelvis

   B) collecting ducts

   C) ureters

   D) glomerulus

6. A patient came to the emergency department complaining of severe lower back pain after a fall. Which vertebrae has the patient most likely injured?

   A) cervical

   B) thoracic

   C) cranial

   D) lumbar

7. Which of the following explains why people experience heartburn?

   A) The esophageal sphincter does not fully close.

   B) The epiglottis remains closed after swallowing.

   C) The stomach was unable to digest its contents.

   D) The pharynx pushes air into the esophagus.

8. A patient with a blocked cerebral artery is experiencing what?

   A) subdural hematoma

   B) myocardial infarction

   C) hemorrhagic stroke

   D) ischemic stroke

9. Which of the following is found in the blood in high levels as a result of muscle fatigue?

   A) ATP

   B) platelets

   C) lactic acid

   D) glucose

10. Which of the following is the largest and outermost part of the brain?

   A) pons

   B) cerebellum

   C) cerebrum

   D) thalamus

11. The hardening and narrowing of the arteries due to plaque buildup is known as

   A) gingivitis.

   B) atherosclerosis.

   C) thrombosis.

   D) melanoma.

12. What is the role of the liver in digestion?

   A) It produces the bile needed to digest fats.

   B) It stores bile produced by the gallbladder.

   C) It regulates feelings of hunger.

   D) It collects the waste that is the end product of digestion.

13. Which of the following hormones is released by the kidneys and helps regulate blood pressure?

   A) renin

   B) calcitriol

   C) cortisol

   D) oxytocin

14. Which of the following is a function of cerebrospinal fluid?

   A) It prevents the layers of the meninges from sticking together.

   B) It mixes with blood to nourish the brain.

   C) It removes waste products from the brain.

   D) It transmits signals to and from the brain.

15. A patient arrives in the emergency room complaining of shortness of breath. A blood test shows that her iron level is low. Which of the following will likely also be decreased?

   A) hemoglobin

   B) plasma

   C) white blood cells

   D) platelets

16. What substance does a Schwann cell secrete that increases the speed of signals traveling to and from neurons?

   A) myelin

   B) cerebrospinal fluid

   C) corpus callosum

   D) collagen

17. Which of the following structures begins the heartbeat by starting an electrical impulse in the right atrium?

   A) atrioventricular (AV) node

   B) sinoatrial (SA) node

   C) bundle of His

   D) mitral valve

18. Which of the following is a function of antibodies during an immune response?

   A) They store information for antibody production when the antigen reappears.

   B) They ingest the pathogen and destroy it.

   C) They produce an enzyme to coat and protect healthy cells.

   D) They bind to the antigen to neutralize pathogens.

19. A patient's blood pressure is 120/80. Which of the following numbers represents the arterial pressure when the ventricles are contracting?

A) 120

B) 80

C) 240

D) 40

20. Which of the following connects the ribs to the sternum?

A) costal cartilage

B) synovial joint

C) cardiac muscle

D) collagen fiber

Answer Key

1. **D) is correct.** The primary purpose of the essay is to inform; its focus is the endocrine system's parts and functions. It is not persuasive or cautionary.

2. **D) is correct.** In the second paragraph, the author writes, "The endocrine system's function is to produce and distribute hormones."

3. **A) is correct.** The answer provides an adequate summary of the passage overall. The other choices only provide specific details from the passage.

4. **B) is correct.** The author writes, "Hormones are also released in humans in moments of fear or anxiety and can trigger the fight-or-flight response." There are no sentences supporting the other claims.

5. **A) is correct.** In the first paragraph, the author writes, "The pituitary gland serves as the 'master gland' of the endocrine system."

6. **A) is correct.** In the second paragraph, the author writes, "When the hormones reach other tissues, they catalyze certain chemical reactions, stimulating various processes or activities." The writer then goes on to describe those activities in detail, making it clear that the hormones caused those events to occur.

7. **A) is correct.** The passage is about how important it is for medical professionals to understand hypoglycemia, especially when it comes to patients who have diabetes. The other answer choices are details from the passage.

8. **B) is correct.** In the second paragraph, the author writes, "You will likely need to help administer glucose to them as soon as possible." In this case, *administer* means to give glucose to a patient.

9. **C) is correct.** This detail is not found in the passage. The passage strongly focuses on patients with diabetes, but it does not state that only those patients are affected by hypoglycemia.

10. **A) is correct.** The text is informative, not persuasive or dramatic. It does not recount a specific event, but simply informs the audience of potential general scenarios.

11. **B) is correct.** In the third paragraph, the author writes, "A blood glucose value of less than 80 milligrams per deciliter can be considered a hypoglycemic episode."

12. **A) is correct.** In the second paragraph, the author states, "When a diabetic patient's blood sugar plummets, their mental state becomes altered. This can lead to unconsciousness or, in more severe cases, a diabetic coma and/or brain damage." The reader can infer from this information that diabetic comas *could* cause *permanent* brain damage.

13. **C) is correct.** The answer provides an adequate summary of the passage overall. The other choices only provide specific details from the passage.

14. **D) is correct.** The primary purpose of the essay is to advise; its focus is communication with patients in crisis. It is not persuasive or cautionary, and it does not tell a story.

15. **B) is correct.** The author writes, "In some cultures, direct eye contact can be unsettling or disrespectful." There are no sentences supporting the other claims.

16. **B) is correct.** In the first paragraph, the author writes, "Communicating with any human being in crisis—whether that crisis is physical or emotional—is going to be more difficult than normal, everyday communication."

17. **D) is correct.** In the last sentence, the author writes, "These tips will help you support people who need clarity and sensitivity."

18. **C) is correct.** In the second paragraph, the author writes, "Your body language speaks volumes." The writer then goes on to detail ways that body language can convey messages (with "posture, hand motions, and gestures").

19. **A) is correct.** In the last paragraph, the author states, "Empathy is crucial for being able to respond properly in social settings." The reader can infer from this information that empathy is a positive quality that people need in order to treat others in a socially acceptable manner.

20. **A) is correct.** The primary purpose of the essay is to inform; its focus is on the definition of empathy. It is not persuasive or advisory. The author does not set out to show that one quality is better than another.

21. **D) is correct.** In the second paragraph, the author defines compassionate empathy as "the ability to control your own emotions while helping others deal with theirs." Readers can infer that this kind of empathy would be useful to medical professionals who have to remain calm in emergencies (when patients and bystanders are often upset).

22. **D) is correct.** In the last paragraph the author writes, "Some people with very strong cognitive empathy may abuse their social understanding as a means to take advantage of others." Earlier the author defines "cognitive empathy" as "the ability to identify and understand the emotions, mental state, or perspective of others."

WRITING

1. **D) is correct.** Sentence 8 is actually a dependent clause.

2. **D) is correct.** Sentence 10 contains an unnecessary word, "that": "the danger of the ice cream headache *that* will certainly not stop people..."

3. **C) is correct.** This sentence explains the "signals" referred to in sentence 9 as "pain." Sentence 10 refers to "wincing," providing a clue that more context about pain is needed. This sentence should be placed after sentence 9.

4. **D) is correct.** Sentence 4 has an unnecessary occurrence of the word *that*: "that the resident bacteria."

5. **C) is correct.** Sentence 5 contains an error in conjugation: "Scientists who been studying." It should be corrected as: "Scientists who *have* been studying."

6. **A) is correct.** This sentence introduces the idea that blood is important for all body systems. The word "other" suggests that more body systems will be discussed. It should be placed after sentence 1 to introduce the ideas in sentences 2, 3, and 4, which refer to specific body systems.

7. **B) is correct.** Sentence 2 contains a verb error. The verb "stimulate" should be the singular "stimulates" to agree with the subject "Blood."

8. **C) is correct.** Sentence 3 contains a verb error: the verb "are" should be the singular "is" to agree with its singular subject, "reason."

9. **D) is correct.** Sentence 11 has no subject: it needs a word like "they" or "men" to be complete.

10. **C) is correct.** Sentence 11 specifically refers to "red meat" and "processed meat." This new sentence should be placed immediately after to provide more information about the consequences of consuming red and processed meat.

11. **C) is correct.** Sentence 3 contains a verb error. The singular verb "is" should be replaced with the plural verb "are" to agree with its plural subject, "People."

12. **D) is correct.** Sentence 9 is missing a subject; it needs a pronoun like "they" to be complete.

13. **B) is correct.** Sentence 5 completes a paragraph about severe cases of autism, and sentence 6 opens a new paragraph describing the "mild end of the spectrum." Placing this new sentence, which also mentions a "spectrum," after sentence 5 is a good way to complete the first paragraph, clarify the needs of people with more severe cases of autism, and transition to the new paragraph.

14. **D) is correct.** In sentence 9, the verb "disrupted" is conjugated incorrectly in the simple past tense. The other verbs in this paragraph are conjugated in the present tense, so it should be too ("disrupts").

15. **A) is correct.** This sentence provides more information about the "environmental factors" mentioned in sentence 1. It also leads to the transition phrase "on the other hand" beginning sentence 3, which then goes on to introduce "extremely dry heat," which is a counter example to the "humid conditions" discussed in the new sentence.

16. **B) is correct.** Sentence 2 requires a subject like the pronoun "it" or the word "inflammation" to be complete.

17. **D) is correct.** In sentence 5, the participle "relieved" should be conjugated "relieve."

18. **C) is correct.** FSH and LH are first mentioned in sentence 3, where the acronyms are spelled out. That is a good clue that the new sentence should be placed after sentence 3, where the terms have been introduced and the acronyms explained. The context and discussion of the action of testosterone suggests the new sentence should precede sentence 4.

19. **D) is correct.** Sentence 7 is not an independent clause; it lacks a subject or an active verb.

20. **B) is correct.** Sentence 2 contains a semicolon that incorrectly connects a dependent clause ("While previous national guidelines focused on the dangers of cholesterol") with an independent clause ("the Obama administration's new guidelines highlighted the dangers of processed sugar.") Semicolons should be used to join two independent clauses.

21. **B) is correct.** In sentence 4, the verb "warning" should be conjugated "warned" to match the subject "guidelines" and be written in the simple past tense to match verbs in the surrounding sentences.

MATHEMATICS

1. **C) is correct.**
   30 minutes = 0.5 hour
   $\frac{13}{0.5} = \frac{x}{7}$
   0.5x = 91
   x = 182

2. **B) is correct.**
   110 lb × $\frac{1 \text{ kg}}{2.2 \text{ lb}}$ ≈ **50 kg**

3. **B) is correct.**
   1800 − 591 = **1209**

4. **B) is correct.**
   26.5 + 18.9 + 35.1 = **80.5**

5. **D) is correct.**
   part = whole × percent
   40 × 0.25 = 10
   40 − 10 = **30**

6. **B) is correct.**
   −2100 + 11,200 = $9100
   $9100 ÷ 2 = **$4550**

7. **D) is correct.**
   If Bob pays $158 per month, the amount he has paid on his bill would be 158 times the number of months, x. Bob's balance will be decreased by the amount he has paid.

8. **A) is correct.**
   $\frac{2 \text{ mg}}{\text{kg}}$ × $\frac{1 \text{ kg}}{2.2 \text{ lb}}$ × 165 lb = **150 mg**

9. **C) is correct.**
   $\frac{2}{7} = \frac{72}{x}$
   2x = 504
   x = 252

10. **B) is correct.**
    3500 ÷ 325 ≈ 10.8, so **10 tablets will stay under the limit**.

11. **A) is correct.**
    $13.50 × 7.5 = **$101.25**

12. **D) is correct.**
    part = whole × percent
    500 × 0.70 = **350**

13. **A) is correct.**
    Let x equal the amount of money Rosie needs to save each week.
    145 + 5x = 520
    5x = 375
    x = 75

14. **C) is correct.**
    F = 1.8C + 32
    F = 1.8(25) + 32
    F = 77°

15. **C) is correct.**
    $\frac{4}{50} = \frac{x}{175}$
    50x = 700
    x = 14

16. **A) is correct.**

$600 - 125 = $ **475**

17. **C) is correct.**

$2\frac{1}{2} + 1\frac{1}{3} = 2\frac{3}{6} + 1\frac{2}{6} = 3\frac{5}{6}$

$8 - 3\frac{5}{6} = \frac{48}{6} - \frac{23}{6} = \frac{25}{6} = $ **$4\frac{1}{6}$**

18. **C) is correct.**

part = whole × percent

$2213 \times 0.44 = 973.72 \approx$ **974**

19. **C) is correct.**

1 week = 7 days

$10 \times 8 \times 7 = $ **560**

20. **C) is correct.**

$\frac{1}{280} = \frac{1.5}{x}$

x = 420

21. **A) is correct.**

$5(x + 3) - 12 = 43$

$5x + 15 - 12 = 43$

$5x + 3 = 43$

$5x = 40$

x = 8

22. **A) is correct.**

$C = \frac{5}{9}(F - 32)$

$C = \frac{5}{9}(98.6 - 32)$

$C = \frac{5}{9}(66.6) = $ **37°**

23. **B) is correct.**

$3\frac{2}{4} + 3\frac{3}{4} + 4 + 4\frac{1}{4} + 4\frac{2}{4} = 18\frac{8}{4} = 18 + 2 = $ **20**

24. **B) is correct.**

$500 - 150 = 350$ mg lost

percent $= \frac{part}{whole}$

$\frac{350}{500} = 0.7 = $ **70%**

25 **C) is correct.**

part = whole × percent

$260 \times 0.05 = 13$

$260 - 13 = $ **247**

26. **A) is correct.**

$1\frac{1}{2}$ years = 18 months

$\frac{18 \times 25}{150} = $ **3**

27. **B) is correct.**

$7\frac{4}{8} + 2\frac{5}{8} + 7\frac{4}{8} = 16\frac{13}{8} = 16 + 1\frac{5}{8} = $ **$17\frac{5}{8}$**

28. **D) is correct.**

1 year = 52 weeks

$1.1 \times 52 = 57.5 \approx$ **58**

SCIENCE

1. **B) is correct.** Red blood cells contain hemoglobin, which has an iron component that transports oxygen. Hemoglobin also makes the red blood cells appear red in color.

2. **C) is correct.** The incus, stapes, and malleus are bones connected to the skull inside the ear. They play an important role in the sense of hearing.

3. **C) is correct.** Calcium is released as bones are degraded, helping balance the calcium level in the body.

4. **B) is correct.** Deoxygenated blood in the heart is delivered to the lungs for gas exchange from the right ventricle.

5. **D) is correct.** The glomerulus is a network of capillaries that begins the filtration process by filtering blood plasma, the result of which is then excreted as urine.

6. **D) is correct.** Lumbar vertebrae are also called the lower back vertebrae.

7. **A) is correct.** The esophagus has a sphincter that should close as food enters the stomach. If it does not fully close, it permits backflow of the stomach contents to the esophagus, causing heartburn.

8. **D) is correct.** The patient is having an ischemic stroke. An ischemic stroke is caused by a blockage of an artery supplying blood to the brain.

9. **C) is correct.** Lactic acid is elevated in the blood when prolonged muscle contraction causes muscle fatigue.

10. **C) is correct.** The cerebrum is the largest and outermost part of the brain.

11. **B) is correct.** Atherosclerosis occurs when arteries are hardened and/or narrowed due to the deposition of fatty plaques on the inner walls.

12. **A) is correct.** The liver produces bile, which is needed for the digestion of fats.

13. **A) is correct.** Renin is released by the kidneys and plays a role in regulating blood pressure.

14. **C) is correct.** Cerebrospinal fluid absorbs waste products from the brain, allowing them to be transferred into the bloodstream.

15. **A) is correct.** Hemoglobin is rich in iron, which allows it to transport oxygen to cells. Thus, a low iron level will likely correspond to a low hemoglobin level.

16. **A) is correct.** Schwann cells secrete myelin, which forms a sheath around the neuron and allows the electrical signal to travel faster.

17. **B) is correct.** The sinoatrial (SA) node starts the electrical conduction pathway for the heart by producing a regular impulse that causes the atria to contract. On an ECG this is reflected by the P wave.

18. **D) is correct.** Antibodies bind to the antigen on the pathogen, neutralizing the pathogen and attracting phagocytes.

19. **A) is correct.** The blood pressure is read as the systolic pressure over the diastolic pressure. During systole, the ventricles are contracting, and blood is being pumped out into the body. The systolic pressure measurement (here, 120), is thus the pressure in the arteries while the ventricles are contracting.

20. **A) is correct.** Costal cartilage connects the ribs to the sternum.

TO ACCESS YOUR SECOND KNAT PRACTICE TEST, FOLLOW THE LINK BELOW:

http://ascenciatestprep.com/knat-online-resources

Made in United States
Orlando, FL
20 October 2023

38077214R00096